Scott Foresman
Science

See learning in a whole new light

Editorial Offices: Glenview, Illinois • Parsippany, New Jersey • New York, New York
Sales Offices: Boston, Massachusetts • Duluth, Georgia • Glenview, Illinois
Coppell, Texas • Sacramento, California • Mesa, Arizona

Series Authors

Dr. Timothy Cooney
Professor of Earth Science and Science Education
University of Northern Iowa (UNI)
Cedar Falls, Iowa

Dr. Jim Cummins
Professor
Department of Curriculum, Teaching, and Learning
The University of Toronto
Toronto, Canada

Dr. James Flood
Distinguished Professor of Literacy and Language
School of Teacher Education
San Diego State University
San Diego, California

Barbara Kay Foots, M.Ed.
Science Education Consultant
Houston, Texas

Dr. M. Jenice Goldston
Associate Professor of Science Education
Department of Elementary Education Programs
University of Alabama
Tuscaloosa, Alabama

Dr. Shirley Gholston Key
Associate Professor of Science Education
Instruction and Curriculum Leadership Department
College of Education
University of Memphis
Memphis, Tennessee

Dr. Diane Lapp
Distinguished Professor of Reading and Language Arts in Teacher Education
San Diego State University
San Diego, California

Sheryl A. Mercier
Classroom Teacher
Dunlap Elementary School
Dunlap, California

Dr. Karen L. Ostlund
UTeach,
College of Natural Sciences
The University of Texas at Austin
Austin, Texas

Dr. Nancy Romance
Professor of Science Education & Principal Investigator
NSF/IERI Science IDEAS Project
Charles E. Schmidt College of Science
Florida Atlantic University
Boca Raton, Florida

Dr. William Tate
Chair and Professor of Education and Applied Statistics
Department of Education
Washington University
St Louis, Missouri

Dr. Kathryn C. Thornton
Professor
School of Engineering and Applied Science
University of Virginia
Charlottesville, Virginia

Dr. Leon Ukens
Professor of Science Education
Department of Physics, Astronomy, and Geosciences
Towson University
Towson, Maryland

Steve Weinberg
Consultant
Connecticut Center for Advanced Technology
East Hartford, Connecticut

ISBN. 0-328-10004-8 (SVE); ISBN. 0-328-15674-4 (A); ISBN: 0-328-15680-9 (B); ISBN: 0-328-15686-8 (C); ISBN: 0-328-15692-2 (D)

5 6 7 8 9 10 V063 12 11 10 09 08 07 06

Consulting Author

Dr. Michael P. Klentschy
Superintendent
El Centro Elementary School District
El Centro, California

Science Content Consultants

Dr. Frederick W. Taylor
Senior Research Scientist
Institute for Geophysics
Jackson School of Geosciences
The University of Texas at Austin
Austin, Texas

Dr. Ruth E. Buskirk
Senior Lecturer
School of Biological Sciences
The University of Texas at Austin
Austin, Texas

Dr. Cliff Frohlich
Senior Research Scientist
Institute for Geophysics
Jackson School of Geosciences
The University of Texas at Austin
Austin, Texas

Brad Armosky
McDonald Observatory
The University of Texas at Austin
Austin, Texas

NASA Content Consultants

Adena Williams Loston, Ph.D.
Chief Education Officer
Office of the Chief Education Officer

Clifford W. Houston, Ph.D.
Deputy Chief Education Officer for Education Programs
Office of the Chief Education Officer

Frank C. Owens
Senior Policy Advisor
Office of the Chief Education Officer

Deborah Brown Biggs
Manager, Education Flight Projects Office
Space Operations Mission Directorate Education Lead

Erika G. Vick
NASA Liaison to Pearson Scott Foresman
Education Flight Projects Office

William E. Anderson
Partnership Manager for Education
Aeronautics Research Mission Directorate

Anita Krishnamurthi
Program Planning Specialist
Space Science Education and Outreach Program

Bonnie J. McClain
Chief of Education
Exploration Systems Mission Directorate

Diane Clayton, Ph.D.
Program Scientist
Earth Science Education

Deborah Rivera
Strategic Alliances Manager
Office of Public Affairs
NASA Headquarters

Douglas D. Peterson
Public Affairs Officer, Astronaut Office
Office of Public Affairs
NASA Johnson Space Center

Nicole Cloutier
Public Affairs Officer, Astronaut Office
Office of Public Affairs
NASA Johnson Space Center

Reviewers

Dr. Maria Aida Alanis
Administrator
Austin ISD
Austin Texas

Melissa Barba
Teacher
Wesley Mathews Elementary
Miami, Florida

Dr. Marcelline Barron
Supervisor/K-12 Math
and Science
Fairfield Public Schools
Fairfield, Connecticut

Jane Bates
Teacher
Hickory Flat Elementary
Canton, Georgia

Denise Bizjack
Teacher
Dr. N. H. Jones
Elementary
Ocala, Florida

Latanya D. Bragg
Teacher
Davis Magnet School
Jackson, Mississippi

Richard Burton
Teacher
George Buck Elementary
School 94
Indianapolis, Indiana

Dawn Cabrera
Teacher
E.W.F. Stirrup School
Miami, Florida

Barbara Calabro
Teacher
Compass Rose Foundation
Ft. Myers, Florida

Lucille Calvin
Teacher
Weddington Math &
Science School
Greenville, Mississippi

Patricia Carmichael
Teacher
Teasley Middle School
Canton, Georgia

Martha Cohn
Teacher
An Wang Middle School
Lowell, Massachusetts

Stu Danzinger
Supervisor
Community Consolidated
School District 59
Arlington Heights, Illinois

Esther Draper
Supervisor/Science Specialist
Belair Math Science
Magnet School
Pine Bluff, Arkansas

Sue Esser
Teacher
Loretto Elementary
Jacksonville, Florida

Dr. Richard Fairman
Teacher
Antioch University
Yellow Springs, Ohio

Joan Goldfarb
Teacher
Indialantic Elementary
Indialantic, Florida

Deborah Gomes
Teacher
A J Gomes Elementary
New Bedford, Massachusetts

Sandy Hobart
Teacher
Mims Elementary
Mims, Florida

Tom Hocker
Teacher/Science Coach
Boston Latin Academy
Dorchester, Massachusetts

Shelley Jaques
Science Supervisor
Moore Public Schools
Moore, Oklahoma

Marguerite W. Jones
Teacher
Spearman Elementary
Piedmont, South Carolina

Kelly Kenney
Teacher
Kansas City Missouri
School District
Kansas City, Missouri

Carol Kilbane
Teacher
Riverside Elementary School
Wichita, Kansas

Robert Kolenda
Teacher
Neshaminy School District
Langhorne, Pennsylvania

Karen Lynn Kruse
Teacher
St. Paul the Apostle
Yonkers, New York

Elizabeth Loures
Teacher
Point Fermin
Elementary School
San Pedro, California

Susan MacDougall
Teacher
Brick Community Primary
Learning Center
Brick, New Jersey

Jack Marine
Teacher
Raising Horizons Quest
Charter School
Philadelphia, Pennsylvania

Nicola Micozzi Jr.
Science Coordinator
Plymouth Public Schools
Plymouth, Massachusetts

Paula Monteiro
Teacher
A J Gomes Elementary
New Bedford, Massachusetts

Tracy Newallis
Teacher
Taper Avenue Elementary
San Pedro, California

Dr. Eugene Nicolo
Supervisor, Science K-12
Moorestown School District
Moorestown, New Jersey

Jeffrey Pastrak
School District of Philadelphia
Philadelphia, Pennsylvania

Helen Pedigo
Teacher
Mt. Carmel Elementary
Huntsville Alabama

Becky Peltonen
Teacher
Patterson Elementary School
Panama City, Florida

Sherri Pensler
Teacher/ESOL
Claude Pepper Elementary
Miami, Florida

Virginia Rogliano
Teacher
Bridgeview Elementary
South Charleston,
West Virginia

Debbie Sanders
Teacher
Thunderbolt Elementary
Orange Park, Florida

Grethel Santamarina
Teacher
E.W.F. Stirrup School
Miami, Florida

Migdalia Schneider
Teacher/Bilingual
Lindell School
Long Beach, New York

Susan Shelly
Teacher
Bonita Springs Elementary
Bonita Springs, Florida

Peggy Terry
Teacher
Madison District 151
South Holland, Illinois

Jane M. Thompson
Teacher
Emma Ward Elementary
Lawrenceburg, Kentucky

Martha Todd
Teacher
W. H. Rhodes Elementary
Milton, Florida

Renee Williams
Teacher
Central Elementary
Bloomfield, New Mexico

Myra Wood
Teacher
Madison Street Academy
Ocala, Florida

Marion Zampa
Teacher
Shawnee Mission
School District
Overland Park, Kansas

Science

See learning in a whole new light

How to Read Science xx

Science Process Skills xxii

Using Scientific Methods xxvi

Science Tools xxviii

Safety in Science xxxii

Unit A Life Science

What are some ways to classify living things?

Chapter 1 • Classifying Plants and Animals

Build Background 2

Lab zone **Directed Inquiry Explore**
What are living things made of?. 4

How to Read Science Compare and Contrast . 5

You Are There! 6

Lesson 1 • What are the building blocks of life? 7

Lesson 2 • How are living things grouped?. 10

Lesson 3 • How are plants classified? 14

Lesson 4 • How are animals classified? 18

Lesson 5 • How do animals adapt? 26

Lab zone **Guided Inquiry Investigate** How can you use a chart to classify a set of objects? 34

Math in Science Symmetry in Nature. 36

Chapter 1 Review and Test Prep. 38

NASA **Career** Biologist 40

Chapter 2 • Energy from Plants

Build Background 42

Lab zone **Directed Inquiry Explore**
How can you show that a plant needs light? 44

How to Read Science Draw Conclusions 45

You Are There! 46

Lesson 1 • What are plants' characteristics? 47

Lesson 2 • What are the parts of plants? 50

Lesson 3 • How do plants reproduce? 54

Lesson 4 • What is the life cycle of a plant? 58

Lab zone **Guided Inquiry Investigate** How can you
grow a potato plant without a seed? 66

Math in Science How Plants Respond to Sunlight 68

Chapter 2 Review and Test Prep 70

NASA **Career** Plant Biologist 72

What features help plants make their own food and reproduce?

Unit A Life Science

How do organisms interact with each other and with their environment?

How do changes in ecosystems affect our world?

Chapter 3 • Ecosystems

Build Background 74

Directed Inquiry **Explore** How can you make a model of an earthworm habitat? 76

How to Read Science **Sequence** 77

You Are There! 78

Lesson 1 • What are the parts of ecosystems? 79

Lesson 2 • How does energy flow in ecosystems? . . . 84

Lesson 3 • How does matter flow in ecosystems? 90

Guided Inquiry **Investigate** What do decomposers do? 96

Math in Science Graphing Populations 98

Chapter 3 Review and Test Prep 100

NASA Ecosystems in Space 102

Biography Rachel Carson 104

Chapter 4 • Changes in Ecosystems

Build Background 106

Directed Inquiry **Explore** What is the effect of crowding on plants? 108

How to Read Science **Cause and Effect** . . . 109

You Are There! 110

Lesson 1 • How are ecosystems balanced?. 111

Lesson 2 • How do organisms interact? 114

Lesson 3 • How do environments change? 118

Lesson 4 • How do people disturb the balance? . . . 124

Guided Inquiry **Investigate** How can a change in the environment affect plant growth? . . . 130

Math in Science Recycling a Fraction 132

Chapter 4 Review and Test Prep 134

NASA **Career** Ecologist. 136

Chapter 5 • Systems of the Human Body

Build Background 138

Lab zone **Directed Inquiry Explore**
How does shape affect bone strength? 140

How to Read Science Draw Conclusions . . . 141

You Are There! 142

Lesson 1 • What are the skeletal and muscular
systems? 143

Lesson 2 • What are the respiratory and circulatory
systems? 148

Lesson 3 • What are the digestive and nervous
systems? 152

Lesson 4 • How does the body defend itself? 156

Lab zone **Guided Inquiry Investigate**
How can some diseases be spread? 162

Math in Science Units of Measure and the Human Body 164

Chapter 5 Review and Test Prep 166

Biography Two Early Doctors 168

Unit A Test Talk 169

Unit A Wrap-Up 170

Lab zone **Full Inquiry Experiment** Do mealworms
prefer damp or dry places? 172

Science Fair Projects Home Sweet Home,
Different Types of Plants, What's Under That Rock?
Inside Information 176

How do the body's smallest and largest parts work together?

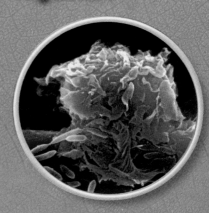

Unit B Earth Science

How does Earth's water affect weather?

Chapter 6 • Water Cycle and Weather

Build Background 178

Directed Inquiry Explore
How can you make fresh water from salt water? . . 180

How to Read Science Cause and Effect . . . 181

You Are There! 182

Lesson 1 • Where is Earth's water? 183

Lesson 2 • How do water and air affect weather? . . 186

Lesson 3 • What are air masses? 190

Lesson 4 • How do we measure and predict weather? 194

Guided Inquiry Investigate
How does water change state? 200

Math in Science Graphing Temperatures 202

Chapter 6 Review and Test Prep 204

NASA Eye in the Sky 206

NASA Biography Joanne Simpson 208

Chapter 7 • Hurricanes and Tornadoes

Build Background 210

Directed Inquiry Explore
How can you make a model of a hurricane? 212

How to Read Science Main Idea and Details 213

You Are There! 214

Lesson 1 • What are hurricanes? 215

Lesson 2 • What are tornadoes? 222

Guided Inquiry Investigate
Where is the hurricane going? 226

Math in Science Ranking Hurricanes 228

Chapter 7 Review and Test Prep 230

Biography Colonel Joseph B. Duckworth 232

How do storms affect Earth's air, water, land, and living things?

Unit B Earth Science

How can rocks tell us about Earth's past, present, and future?

How is Earth's surface shaped and reshaped?

Chapter 8 • Minerals and Rocks

Build Background 234

Lab zone Directed Inquiry **Explore**
How can you classify rocks and minerals? 236

How to Read Science **Summarize** 237

You Are There! 238

Lesson 1 • What are minerals? 239

Lesson 2 • How are sedimentary rocks formed? . . . 242

Lesson 3 • What are igneous and metamorphic rocks? 246

Lab zone Guided Inquiry **Investigate**
What properties can you use to identify minerals? . 250

Math in Science Large Numbers in Science 252

Chapter 8 Review and Test Prep 254

NASA **Biography** Doug Ming 256

Chapter 9 • Changes to Earth's Surface

Build Background 258

Lab zone Directed Inquiry **Explore**
How can you observe a mineral wear away? . . . 260

How to Read Science **Compare and Contrast** 261

You Are There! 262

Lesson 1 • How does Earth's surface wear away? . . 263

Lesson 2 • How do weathered materials move? . . . 266

Lesson 3 • How can Earth's surface
change rapidly? 270

Lab zone Guided Inquiry **Investigate**
How does distance change earthquake effects? . . 274

Math in Science Comparing Sizes of Earthquakes . . 276

Chapter 9 Review and Test Prep 278

Career Oceanographer 280

Chapter 10 • Using Natural Resources

Build Background 282

Lab zone **Directed Inquiry Explore**
How can you collect sunlight? 284

How to Read Science Cause and Effect . . . 285

You Are There! 286

Lesson 1 • What are natural resources? 287

Lesson 2 • How are resources used for energy? . . . 292

Lab zone **Guided Inquiry Investigate**
How can you observe a "fossil fuel" being formed?. 298

Math in Science Water Use 300

Chapter 10 Review and Test Prep 302

Career Auto Engineer 304

Unit B Test Talk 305

Unit B Wrap-Up 306

Lab zone **Full Inquiry Experiment**
What affects how rain erodes soil? 308

Science Fair Projects The Answer Is Blowing
in the Wind, Acid Rain, Please Pass the Salt Water,
The Last Straw 312

How can living things always have the natural resources they need?

How can matter be compared, measured, and combined?

Chapter 11 • Properties of Matter

Build Background 314

Lab zone **Directed Inquiry Explore**
What properties cause liquids to form layers? . . . 316

How to Read Science Compare and Contrast 317

You Are There! 318

Lesson 1 • What is matter? 319

Lesson 2 • How is matter measured? 322

Lesson 3 • How do substances mix? 328

Lesson 4 • How does matter change? 332

Lab zone **Guided Inquiry Investigate**
How can you change the properties of glue? 338

Math in Science Comparing Densities 340

Chapter 11 Review and Test Prep 342

NASA **Career** Analytical Chemist 344

How does heat energy move from one object to another?

Chapter 12 • Heat

Build Background 346

Lab zone **Directed Inquiry Explore**
How can you make things warmer? 348

How to Read Science Cause and Effect . . . 349

You Are There! 350

Lesson 1 • Why does matter have energy? 351

Lesson 2 • How does heat move? 354

Lab zone **Guided Inquiry Investigate** How are
thermal energy and temperature different? 360

Math in Science Using Temperature Scales 362

Chapter 12 Review and Test Prep 364

NASA Managing Heat Transfer 366

Biography Max Planck 368

Chapter 13 • Electricity and Magnetism

Build Background 370

Directed Inquiry Explore
How can static electricity affect objects? 372

How to Read Science Cause and Effect . . . 373

You Are There! 374

Lesson 1 • How does matter become charged? 375

Lesson 2 • How do electric charges flow? 378

Lesson 3 • What are magnetic fields? 382

Lesson 4 • How is electricity transformed
to magnetism? 386

Lesson 5 • How is magnetism transformed
to electricity? 390

Guided Inquiry Investigate
What is an electromagnet? 394

Math in Science Using Numbers to Represent
Electrical Charges 396

Chapter 13 Review and Test Prep 398

Biography William Gilbert 400

What are some ways that energy can be changed from one type to another?

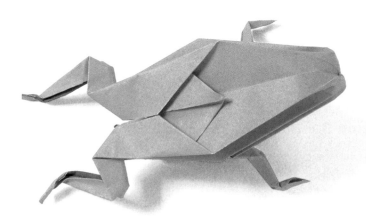

Unit C · Physical Science

How do sound and light travel?

What causes motion and how does it affect us?

Chapter 14 • Sound and Light

Build Background 402

Directed Inquiry **Explore**
What makes sound change? 404

How to Read Science **Draw Conclusions** . . . 405

You Are There! 406

Lesson 1 • What is sound energy? 407

Lesson 2 • How is sound made? 412

Lesson 3 • What is light energy? 416

Lesson 4 • How do light and matter interact? 420

Guided Inquiry **Investigate**
How is light reflected and refracted? 426

Math in Science Comparing Speeds 428

Chapter 14 Review and Test Prep 430

Career Optometrist 432

Chapter 15 • Objects in Motion

Build Background 434

Directed Inquiry **Explore**
What can change a marble's speed? 436

How to Read Science **Sequence** 437

You Are There! 438

Lesson 1 • What is motion? 439

Lesson 2 • How does force affect moving objects? . . 442

Lesson 3 • How are force, mass, and energy related? 446

Guided Inquiry **Investigate**
How does friction affect motion? 450

Math in Science Relating Distance, Speed, and Time . 452

Chapter 15 Review and Test Prep 454

Career Space Engineer 456

xvi

Chapter 16 • Simple Machines

Build Background 458

Lab zone **Directed Inquiry Explore**
How can a machine ring a bell?. 460

How to Read Science Summarize 461

You Are There! 462

Lesson 1 • What is a machine? 463

Lesson 2 • How can machines work together? 468

Lab zone **Guided Inquiry Investigate**
What tasks can a machine do? 474

Math in Science Using Half the Force 476

Chapter 16 Review and Test Prep 478

Biography Archimedes 480

Unit C Test Talk 481

Unit C Wrap-Up 482

Lab zone **Full Inquiry Experiment**
How is motion affected by mass? 484

Science Fair Projects A Pinhole Camera,
Build a Better Door Opener, Battery Power. 488

How do simple machines make work easier?

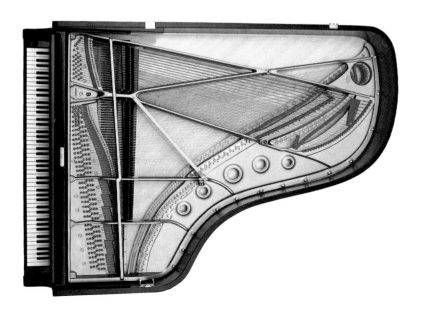

Unit D Space and Technology

How are cycles on Earth affected by the Sun and the Moon?

How is Earth different from other planets in our solar system?

Chapter 17 • Earth's Cycles

Build Background 490

Directed Inquiry **Explore**
What is the shape of a planet's path? 492

How to Read Science **Cause and Effect** . . . 493

You Are There! 494

Lesson 1 • How does Earth move? 495

Lesson 2 • What patterns can you see in the sky? . . 500

Guided Inquiry **Investigate**
How can you make a star finder? 506

Math in Science Comparing Hours of Daylight 508

Chapter 17 Review and Test Prep 510

Biography Robert B. Lee III 512

Chapter 18 • Inner and Outer Planets

Build Background 514

Directed Inquiry **Explore**
How can you compare the sizes of planets? 516

How to Read Science **Predicting** 517

You Are There! 518

Lesson 1 • What makes up the universe? 519

Lesson 2 • What are the inner planets? 522

Lesson 3 • What do we know about Jupiter, Saturn, and Uranus? 528

Lesson 4 • What do we know about Neptune, Pluto, and beyond? 534

Guided Inquiry **Investigate**
How does spinning affect a planet's shape? 538

Math in Science Using Data About Planets 540

Chapter 18 Review and Test Prep 542

Biography Nicolaus Copernicus 544

Chapter 19 • Effects of Technology

Build Background 546

Lab zone **Directed Inquiry Explore**
How do communications satellites work? 548

How to Read Science Main Idea and Details . 549

You Are There! 550

Lesson 1 • How does technology affect our lives? . . . 551

Lesson 2 • How has technology changed
communication and transportation? 556

Lab zone **Guided Inquiry Investigate**
Why are satellite antennas curved? 560

Math in Science Scale Models and Scale Drawings . . 562

Chapter 19 Review and Test Prep 564

NASA Telemedicine 566

Biography Otis Boykin 568

How do the devices and products of technology affect the way we live?

Unit D Test Talk 569

Unit D Wrap-Up 570

Lab zone **Full Inquiry Experiment** How does payload
affect the distance a model rocket can travel? . . . 572

Science Fair Projects How Heavy Is Heavy?
Objects in Space, Phases of the Moon,
What Time Is It? 576

Metric and Customary Measurement EM1

Glossary EM2

Index EM10

Credits EM31

How to Read Science

A page like the one below is found near the beginning of each chapter. It shows you how to use a reading skill that will help you understand what you read.

Before Reading

Before you read the chapter, read the Build Background page and think about how to answer the question. Recall what you already know as you answer the question. Work with a partner to make a list of what you already know. Then read the How to Read Science page.

Target Reading Skill
Each page has one target reading skill. The reading skill corresponds with a process skill in the Directed Inquiry activity on the facing page. The reading skill will be useful as you read science.

Real-World Connection
Each page has an example of something you might read. It also connects with the Directed Inquiry activity.

Graphic Organizer
A useful strategy for understanding anything you read is to make a graphic organizer. A graphic organizer can help you think about the information and how parts of it relate to each other. Each reading skill has a graphic organizer.

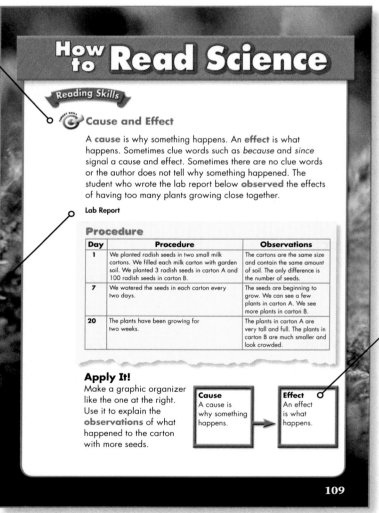

How to Read Science

Reading Skills

Cause and Effect

A **cause** is why something happens. An **effect** is what happens. Sometimes clue words such as *because* and *since* signal a cause and effect. Sometimes there are no clue words or the author does not tell why something happened. The student who wrote the lab report below **observed** the effects of having too many plants growing close together.

Lab Report

Procedure

Day	Procedure	Observations
1	We planted radish seeds in two small milk cartons. We filled each milk carton with garden soil. We planted 3 radish seeds in carton A and 100 radish seeds in carton B.	The cartons are the same size and contain the same amount of soil. The only difference is the number of seeds.
7	We watered the seeds in each carton every two days.	The seeds are beginning to grow. We can see a few plants in carton A. We see more plants in carton B.
20	The plants have been growing for two weeks.	The plants in carton A are very tall and full. The plants in carton B are much smaller and look crowded.

Apply It!
Make a graphic organizer like the one at the right. Use it to explain the **observations** of what happened to the carton with more seeds.

Cause	Effect
A cause is why something happens.	An effect is what happens.

109

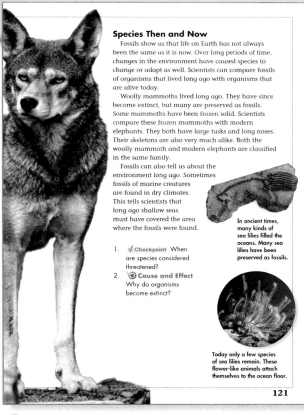

Species Then and Now

Fossils show us that life on Earth has not always been the same as it is now. Over long periods of time, changes in the environment have caused species to change or adapt as well. Scientists can compare fossils of organisms that lived long ago with organisms that are alive today.

Woolly mammoths lived long ago. They have since become extinct, but many are preserved as fossils. Some mammoths have been frozen solid. Scientists compare these frozen mammoths with modern elephants. They both have large tusks and long noses. Their skeletons are also very much alike. Both the woolly mammoth and modern elephants are classified in the same family.

Fossils can also tell us about the environment long ago. Sometimes fossils of marine creatures are found in dry climates. This tells scientists that long ago shallow seas must have covered the area where the fossils were found.

In ancient times, many kinds of sea lilies filled the oceans. Many sea lilies have been preserved as fossils.

1. √ **Checkpoint** When are species considered threatened?
2. ⟳ **Cause and Effect** Why do organisms become extinct?

Today only a few species of sea lilies remain. These flower-like animals attach themselves to the ocean floor.

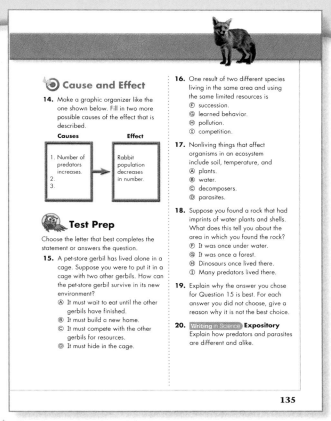

⟳ Cause and Effect

14. Make a graphic organizer like the one shown below. Fill in two more possible causes of the effect that is described.

Causes		Effect
1. Number of predators increases. 2. 3.	→	Rabbit population decreases in number.

🦉 Test Prep

Choose the letter that best completes the statement or answers the question.

15. A pet-store gerbil has lived alone in a cage. Suppose you were to put it in a cage with two other gerbils. How can the pet-store gerbil survive in its new environment?
    - Ⓐ It must wait to eat until the other gerbils have finished.
    - Ⓑ It must build a new home.
    - Ⓒ It must compete with the other gerbils for resources.
    - Ⓓ It must hide in the cage.

16. One result of two different species living in the same area and using the same limited resources is
    - Ⓕ succession.
    - Ⓖ learned behavior.
    - Ⓗ pollution.
    - Ⓘ competition.

17. Nonliving things that affect organisms in an ecosystem include soil, temperature, and
    - Ⓐ plants.
    - Ⓑ water.
    - Ⓒ decomposers.
    - Ⓓ parasites.

18. Suppose you found a rock that had imprints of water plants and shells. What does this tell you about the area in which you found the rock?
    - Ⓕ It was once under water.
    - Ⓖ It was once a forest.
    - Ⓗ Dinosaurs once lived there.
    - Ⓘ Many predators lived there.

19. Explain why the answer you chose for Question 15 is best. For each answer you did not choose, give a reason why it is not the best choice.

20. **Writing in Science** **Expository** Explain how predators and parasites are different and alike.

⟳ During Reading

As you read the lesson, use the checkpoint to check your understanding. Some checkpoints ask you to use the reading target skill.

⟳ After Reading

After you have read the chapter, think about what you found out. Exchange ideas with a partner. Compare the list you made before you read the chapter with what you learned by reading it. Answer the questions in the Chapter Review. One question uses the reading target skill.

Graphic Organizers

These are the target reading skills and graphic organizers that appear in this book.

☐→☐ Cause and Effect	Draw Conclusions
⬭ Compare and Contrast	Summarize
Sequence	Main Idea and Details
Predict	

Science Process Skills

Investigating the Everglades

Scientists use process skills when they investigate places or events. You will use these skills when you do the activities in this book. Which process skills might scientists use when they investigate the animals and plants of the Everglades?

Observe
A scientist investigating the Everglades observes many things. You use your senses too to find out about other objects, events, or living things.

Classify
Scientists classify living things in the Everglades according to their characteristics. When you classify, you arrange or sort objects, events, or living things.

Estimate and Measure
Scientists might estimate the size of a tree in the Everglades. When they estimate, they tell what they think an object's size, mass, or temperature will measure. Then they measure these factors in units.

Infer
During an investigation, scientists infer what they think is happening, based on what they already know.

Predict
Before they go into the Everglades, scientists tell what they think they will find.

Make and Use Models
Scientists might make and use models, such as maps, to help plan where to go during an investigation.

Make Operational Definitions
When scientists make operational definitions, they describe objects or events based on their experiences.

Science Process Skills

Form Questions and Hypotheses
Think of a statement that you can test to solve a problem or answer a question about the animals you see in the Everglades.

If you were a scientist, you might explore further into the Everglades. What questions might you have about the living things you see? How would you use process skills in your investigation?

Collect Data
Scientists collect data from their observations in the Everglades. They put the data into charts or tables.

Interpret Data
Scientists use the information they collected to solve problems or answer questions.

Investigate and Experiment
As the scientists explore the Everglades, they investigate and experiment to test a hypothesis.

Identify and Control Variables
As scientsts perform an experiment, they identify and control the variables so that they test only one thing at a time.

Communicate
Scientists use words, pictures, charts, and graphs to share information about their investigation.

Using Scientific Methods for Science Inquiry

Scientists use scientific methods as they work. Scientific methods are organized ways to answer questions and solve problems. Scientific methods include the steps shown here. Scientists might not use all the steps. They might not use the steps in this order. You will use scientific methods when you do the **Full Inquiry** activity at the end of each unit. You also will use scientific methods when you do Science Fair Projects.

Ask a question.

You might have a question about something you observe.

What material is best for keeping heat in water?

State your hypothesis.

A hypothesis is a possible answer to your question.

If I wrap the jar in fake fur, then the water will stay warmer longer.

Identify and control variables.

Variables are things that can change. For a fair test, you choose just one variable to change. Keep all other variables the same.

Test other materials. Put the same amount of warm water in other jars that are the same type, size, and shape.

Test your hypothesis.

Make a plan to test your hypothesis. Collect materials and tools. Then follow your plan.

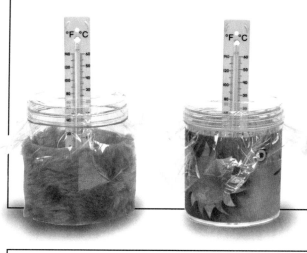

Collect and record your data.

Keep good records of what you do and find out. Use tables and pictures to help.

Interpret your data.

Organize your notes and records to make them clear. Make diagrams, charts, or graphs to help.

State your conclusion.

Your conclusion is a decision you make based on your data. Communicate what you found out. Tell whether or not your data supported your hypothesis.

Fake fur did the best job of keeping the water warm.

Go further.

Use what you learn. Think of new questions to test or better ways to do a test.

Ask a Question

State Your Hypothesis

Identify and Control Variables

Test Your Hypothesis

Collect and Record Your Data

Interpret Your Data

State Your Conclusion

Go Further

Science Tools

Scientists use many different kinds of tools. Tools can make objects appear larger. They can help you measure volume, temperature, length, distance, and mass. Tools can help you figure out amounts and analyze your data. Tools can also help you find the latest scientific information.

You can use a **telescope** to help you see the stars. Some telescopes have special mirrors that gather lots of light and magnify things that are very far away, such as stars and planets.

You can use a **magnifying lens** or **hand lens** to make objects appear larger and to show more detail than you could see with just your eyes. A **hand lens** doesn't enlarge things as much as microscopes do, but it is easier to carry on a field trip.

A **metric tape** can be used like a meterstick or ruler to measure length, but it is flexible to measure around objects.

Pictures taken with a **camera** record what something looks like. You can compare pictures of the same object to show how the object might have changed over time.

Microscopes use several lenses to make objects appear much larger, so you can see more detail.

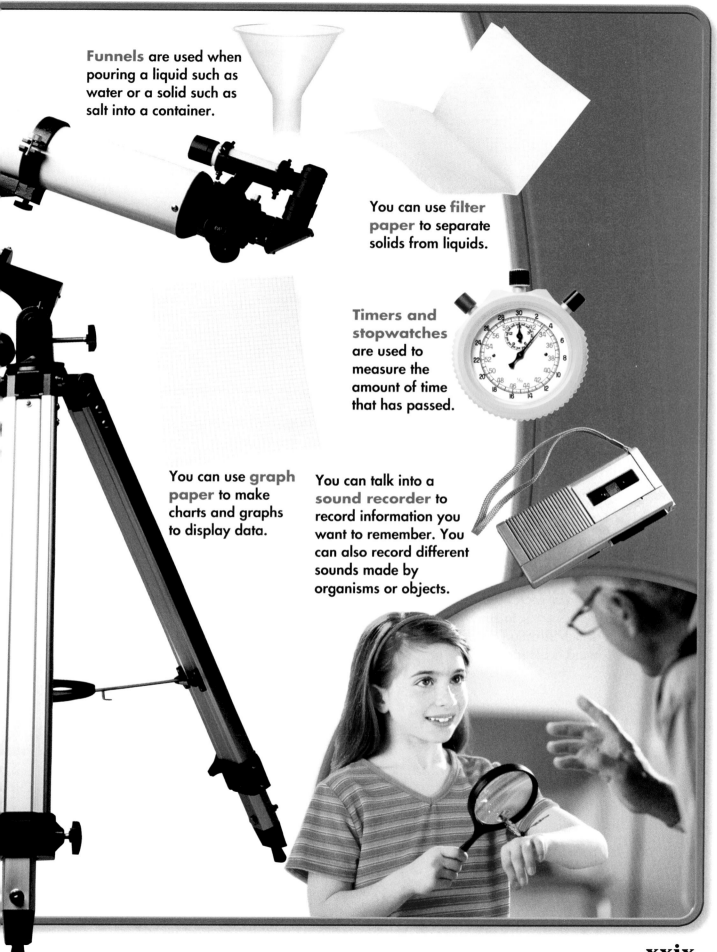

Funnels are used when pouring a liquid such as water or a solid such as salt into a container.

You can use **filter paper** to separate solids from liquids.

Timers and stopwatches are used to measure the amount of time that has passed.

You can use **graph paper** to make charts and graphs to display data.

You can talk into a **sound recorder** to record information you want to remember. You can also record different sounds made by organisms or objects.

Science Tools

You use a **thermometer** to measure temperature. Many thermometers have both Fahrenheit and Celsius scales. Scientists usually use only the Celsius scale. Thermometers also can be used to help measure a gain or loss of energy.

Scientists use **barometers** to measure air pressure, which can be a good indicator of weather patterns.

A **weather vane** is used to determine wind direction.

You can look at a **wind sock** to see which direction the wind is blowing.

A **rain gauge** is used to measure the amount of rain that has fallen.

Terminals are parts of batteries or other devices to which wires are attached to form an electric circuit.

A **multimeter** can measure several characteristics of electricity.

You can use **computers** in many ways, such as to help collect, record, and analyze data.

Calculators make analyzing data easier and faster.

Safety in Science

Scientists know they must work safely when doing experiments. You need to be careful when doing science activities too. Follow these safety rules.

- Read the activity carefully before you start.
- Listen to the teacher's instructions. Ask questions about things you do not understand.
- Wear safety goggles when needed.
- Keep your work area neat and clean. Clean up spills right away.
- Never taste or smell substances unless directed to do so by your teacher.
- Handle sharp items and other equipment carefully.
- Use chemicals carefully.
- Help keep plants and animals that you use safe.
- Tell your teacher if there is an accident or you see something that looks unsafe.
- Put materials away when you finish.
- Dispose of chemicals properly.
- Wash your hands well when you are finished.

Chapter 17

Earth's Cycles

You Will Discover

- different ways Earth moves.
- what causes the seasons.
- why the shape of the Moon appears to change throughout the month.
- what groups of stars can be seen in the sky.

online
Student Edition
sfsuccessnet.com

489

How are cycles on Earth affected by the Sun and the Moon?

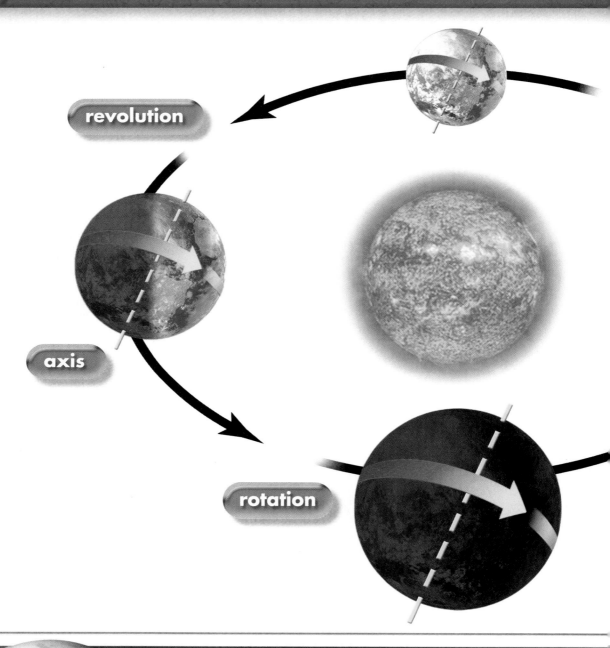

revolution

axis

rotation

eclipse

lunar eclipse

490

orbit

ellipse

Chapter 17 Vocabulary

axis page 496

rotation page 496

revolution page 498

orbit page 498

ellipse page 498

eclipse page 502

lunar eclipse page 502

solar eclipse page 503

constellation page 504

solar eclipse

constellation

Explore What is the shape of a planet's path?

Materials

paper

heavy cardboard

tape

2 pins

metric ruler

piece of string

What to Do

1. Tape the paper onto the cardboard. Stick a pin in the center. Tie a knot to make a loop of string. Put the loop over the pin. Use a pencil and the string to draw a circle. Hold the pencil upright against the stretched string as you draw your circle.

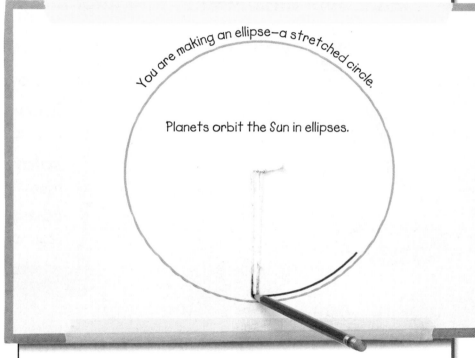
You are making an ellipse—a stretched circle.

Planets orbit the Sun in ellipses.

2. Put a second pin about 5 mm away from the first pin. Put the loop of string over both pins. Try to draw another circle. **Observe** the shape carefully. Is the length from the center to the edge the same in all directions?

Explain Your Results

Predict the effect of moving the second pin farther from the center. How would the new ellipse be different?

Process Skills

Scientific **predictions** are predictions that can be tested.

How to Read Science

Cause and Effect

Linking **causes and effects** can help you understand what you read. Sometimes cause-and-effect relationships that you know can help you **predict** other events.

Science Magazine Article

Earth spins like a top. At the same time, it travels around the Sun. However, Earth's axis—the imaginary line it spins around—is tilted compared with Earth's path around the Sun.

Each half of Earth tilts toward the Sun for about half of the year. Sunlight reaching that hemisphere heats Earth more. Also, because the Sun is higher in the sky, there are more hours of daylight. So, the temperatures are higher. During the rest of the year, this half of Earth tilts away from the Sun. There are fewer hours of daylight, and temperatures are lower.

As Earth revolves around the Sun, these differences in temperature and the hours of daylight cause the seasons.

Apply It!

Use **causes and effects** in the science magazine article to answer the questions or make a **prediction.**

- How does Earth's tilt affect the amount of sunlight that heats the half of Earth that is tilted toward the Sun?

- How does the position of the Sun in the sky affect the number of daylight hours?

- When the Earth has moved to the opposite side of its orbit, which hemisphere is then tilted toward the Sun?

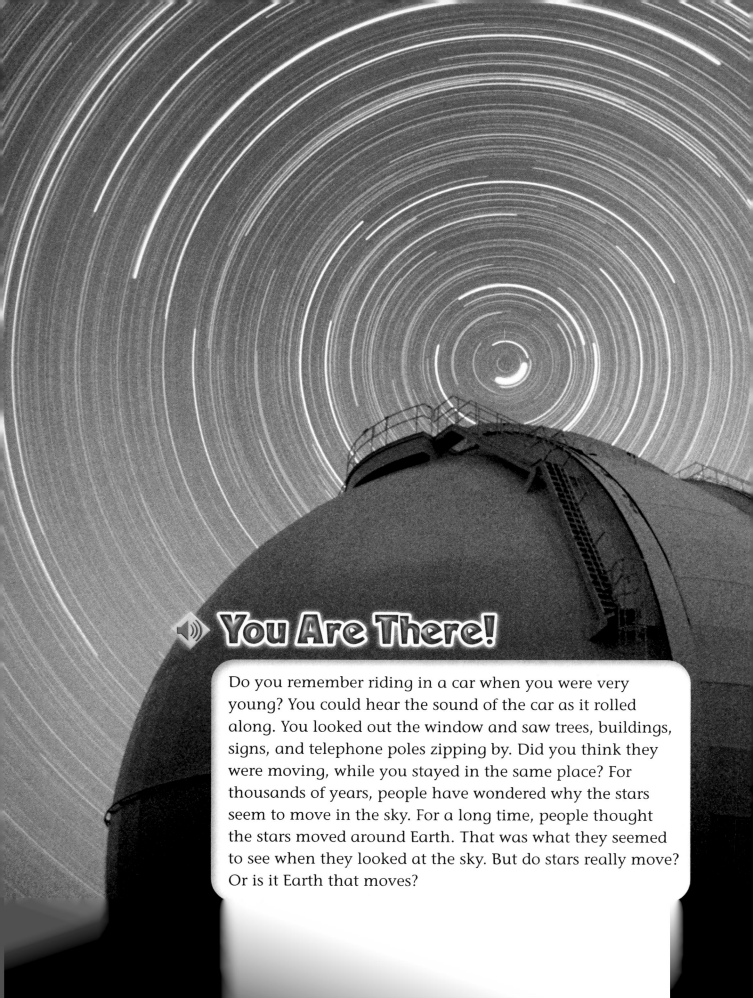

🔊 You Are There!

Do you remember riding in a car when you were very young? You could hear the sound of the car as it rolled along. You looked out the window and saw trees, buildings, signs, and telephone poles zipping by. Did you think they were moving, while you stayed in the same place? For thousands of years, people have wondered why the stars seem to move in the sky. For a long time, people thought the stars moved around Earth. That was what they seemed to see when they looked at the sky. But do stars really move? Or is it Earth that moves?

Lesson 1

How does Earth move?

Earth spins like a top as it circles around and around the Sun. Earth is tipped to one side as it moves. This tilt causes the changing seasons.

Earth Seems to Stand Still

Everyone agrees that Earth doesn't seem to move. You can't sense its movement because you are moving right along with it! Everything on Earth moves at the same speed as the part of Earth just below it. Another reason you don't sense Earth's motion is that it moves steadily and smoothly.

Even though you can't feel Earth's motion, you can find some clues to it. One clue is that to people on Earth, the Sun and the stars seem to move across the sky. This happens because Earth is turning. Another clue is that the seasons change during the year for most places away from the equator. The equator is the imaginary line that divides the north and south halves of Earth. In some areas, the difference in seasons is more dramatic than in other regions. The seasonal changes are partly caused by the way Earth moves around the Sun.

Today, scientists use telescopes, cameras, and computers to study how the stars and other objects in the sky seem to move. We have learned a lot about the stars since people looked at the sky thousands of years ago.

1. **✓ Checkpoint** Why does Earth seem to be standing still?
2. **Social Studies** in Science Use the Internet or other sources to find out about early people whose ideas about the Sun, the stars, and the Moon had an effect on their rituals or customs. Write a report explaining what you learned.

Earth's Rotation

If you have ridden on a merry-go-round, you know that it turns around a pole that runs through its center. Earth turns around its **axis,** an imaginary line that goes through its center. Earth's axis passes through the North Pole, the center of Earth, and the South Pole.

The spinning of Earth around its axis is called its **rotation.** Each time Earth makes a full turn around its axis, it has made one rotation. Earth takes 23 hours and 56 minutes to make one rotation. When Earth rotates, it turns from west to east. Because of Earth's rotation, objects such as the Sun and the other stars appear to move from east to west in the sky.

Why Shadows Change

Another result of Earth's rotation is that shadows change their positions and sizes during the day. When light shines on an object and does not pass through it, the object casts a shadow. As Earth rotates, sunlight shines on an object from different angles. The length and position of the object's shadow changes. Earth's rotation also causes day to change into night and night into day. When a place on Earth is turned toward the Sun, it has daytime. It has nighttime when it is turned away from the Sun.

Like the Sun, the other stars appear to move in the sky from east to west. You cannot see these stars in the daytime because the light from the Sun is too bright. If you watch for several nights, if the sky is clear, and if you are in a place that does not have many bright lights, you can see that stars appear to change their positions in the sky.

An object's shadow is longest in the morning and in the evening when the Sun is low in the sky. It is shortest at the middle of the day, when the Sun is overhead. Which photo was taken closer to noon?

Daylight Hours

The number of hours of daylight at every place on Earth changes during the year. The graph shows the number of hours of sunlight in the middle of the month in Sarasota, Florida.

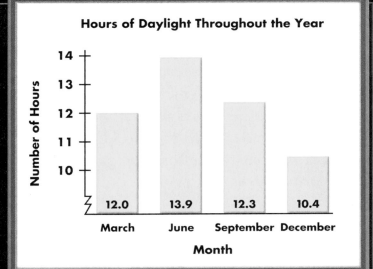

Hours of Daylight Throughout the Year

Number of Hours

March	June	September	December
12.0	13.9	12.3	10.4

Month

Viewed from the same location on Earth, the Sun's position changes depending on the time of day and the time of year.

Evening ← Noon — Morning

Summer

Winter

Earth rotates from west to east as it spins around its axis.

1. **Checkpoint** Why do the Sun and the stars appear to move from east to west in the sky?

2. **Writing in Science** **Expository** In your **science journal** write an article for a newspaper's weather page that explains how and why shadows change their positions during the day. Include some examples from things around you.

497

Earth's Revolution

As Earth rotates, it travels around the Sun. The movement of one object around another is a **revolution.** A complete trip around the Sun by Earth is one revolution. The path Earth follows as it revolves around the Sun is its **orbit.**

Earth takes 1 year, or about 365 days, to complete 1 revolution. During that year, Earth and everything on it travel about 940,000,000 kilometers at an average speed of about 107,000 kilometers per hour.

Earth's orbit is an **ellipse.** An ellipse is like a circle stretched out in opposite directions. As Earth moves in its orbit, its distance from the Sun changes. Earth is farther from the Sun in some parts of its orbit. It is closer to the Sun in other parts.

Gravity is a force that pulls two objects toward each other. It can act at a distance. The gravity between Earth and the Sun keeps Earth revolving around the Sun. Without gravity, Earth would fly off into space. If Earth stopped moving, the attraction between Earth and the Sun would make them crash into each other.

When the North Pole tilts toward the Sun, the Northern Hemisphere gets more direct sunlight.

The midnight Sun moves across the sky just above the horizon.

Earth's Tilted Axis

Earth's axis is always tilted. As Earth revolves around the Sun, its axis is always tilted in the same direction. The end of the axis at the North Pole currently points toward Polaris, the North Star. This tilt affects how places on Earth receive sunlight. In different parts of Earth's orbit, different places directly face the Sun.

In late June, the Northern Hemisphere half of Earth, tilts toward the Sun. It is summer, and daylight is longer than night. But it is winter in the Southern Hemisphere. Nights are longer than daylight. In late December, the Southern Hemisphere tilts toward the Sun. Now, it is winter in the Northern Hemisphere and summer in the Southern Hemisphere. Earth's axis is not tilted toward the Sun in spring and fall. The lengths of daylight and night are more nearly equal in spring and fall.

The Northern Hemisphere gets more direct sunlight when it tilts toward the Sun. Direct sunlight heats this hemisphere more, and daylight lasts longer. As a result, temperatures are higher. It is summer. At the same time, the Southern Hemisphere tilts away from the Sun. The days are shorter, and temperatures are lower. It is winter. In spring and fall, temperatures are more moderate in both hemispheres.

When the North Pole tilts away from the Sun, the rays strike the Northern Hemisphere at a lower angle, and the Southern Hemisphere gets more direct sunlight.

✓ Lesson Checkpoint

1. Why is it summer in the Northern Hemisphere when it is winter in the Southern Hemisphere?
2. ⟳ **Cause and Effect** Explain what causes Earth's seasons.

The Midnight Sun

For several weeks of a hemisphere's summer, the area near the pole gets some sunlight all day and all night. The "midnight Sun" takes an almost circular path close to the horizon. The Sun does not rise high overhead and it does not set. During summer in the Northern Hemisphere, the midnight Sun is seen north of the Arctic Circle. During summer in the Southern Hemisphere, the midnight Sun is seen south of the Antarctic Circle.

Lesson 2

What patterns can you see in the sky?

As the Moon orbits Earth, the same side of the Moon always faces Earth.

You see stars in different parts of the night sky as Earth rotates on its axis and revolves around the Sun. The Moon revolves around Earth. It also rotates on its own axis. All these movements cause changes in the patterns that you see in the sky.

Sun, Moon, and Earth

Sometimes you can see the Moon at night. Sometimes you can even see it during the day. The Moon looks as if it is shining with its own light, just as the Sun does. But the Moon does not really produce its own light. You can see the Moon because sunlight reflects off the Moon's surface.

Like Earth's orbit around the Sun, the Moon's orbit around Earth is shaped like an ellipse. The gravity between the Moon and Earth keeps the Moon in its orbit. Because it moves, the Moon stays in its orbit and doesn't crash into Earth. The Moon makes a complete revolution around Earth in about 27.3 days.

Like Earth, the Moon rotates around its axis. Each time it rotates once around its axis, it revolves once around Earth. As a result, the same side of the Moon is always facing Earth. That is the only side you can see from Earth.

New Moon: Since the Moon's dark, unlighted side faces Earth, you can't see a new Moon. The new Moon begins a new set of phases.

Crescent: A sliver of lighted Moon appears.

First quarter: One half of the lighted half of the Moon, or one quarter of the Moon is visible.

The Phases of the Moon

If you look at the Moon at different times of the month, its shape appears to change. Half of the Moon faces the Sun, and sunlight is reflected from the surface of that half. When the lighted half of the Moon directly faces Earth, the Moon appears as a full circle of light. It is called a full Moon.

We see a full Moon only briefly each time the Moon revolves around Earth. The rest of the time, only part of the lighted half of the Moon faces Earth. Then, you can see only part of the full circle of light. For a short time, you cannot see any of the lighted part of the Moon. So, you do not see the Moon at all. Between the times you see the full Moon and the time you can't see any Moon at all, the Moon appears to have different shapes. All the Moon's shapes are called the phases of the Moon.

Full Moon: The entire half of the Moon that faces Earth is lighted. You see the Moon as a full circle. A full Moon appears about a week after the first quarter.

Last quarter: Gradually, you see less and less of the Moon. About a week after the full Moon, the Moon appears as half of a circle. You see half of the lighted half, or one quarter of the entire Moon.

1. ✓Checkpoint What causes the apparent repeated changes of the Moon's shape?
2. Math in Science About how many times does the Moon revolve around Earth in one year?

Eclipses

An **eclipse** occurs when one object in space gets between the Sun and another object, and casts its shadow on the other object. This occurs when the Moon passes through Earth's shadow and when the Moon's shadow falls on part of Earth.

Most of the time, reflected sunlight lights up the Moon. However, during some full moons, the Moon and the Sun are on exactly opposite sides of Earth. Often, the Moon passes above or below Earth's shadow. But sometimes it passes through Earth's shadow. Then a **lunar eclipse** occurs.

If only part of the Moon is in Earth's shadow during the eclipse, the Moon might look as if something took a bite out of it. This is a partial eclipse. If the whole Moon is in Earth's shadow, the eclipse is a total lunar eclipse. A lunar eclipse can last as long as 100 minutes. It can happen several times in the same year. Each eclipse is visible only in certain places. Where on Earth the eclipse can be viewed depends on the Moon's position in Earth's shadow.

During a total lunar eclipse, the Moon does not disappear completely. Earth's atmosphere bends and scatters some sunlight, so some of the Sun's rays reach the Moon. The Moon appears to be copper colored.

During a lunar eclipse, the Moon moves into and out of Earth's shadow.

Light from the Sun

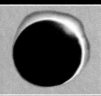
During a total solar eclipse, the Sun may not be visible at all. Sometimes in a solar eclipse a thin, bright ring of sunlight appears to circle the Moon.

Solar Eclipses

A **solar eclipse** occurs when the Moon passes between the Sun and Earth and casts its shadow on Earth. Notice in the picture that the Moon's shadow covers only a small part of Earth. A solar eclipse can be seen only at the places on Earth where the Moon casts its shadow.

During a total solar eclipse, the day can become as dark as night. Total solar eclipses last up to 7.5 minutes. Solar eclipses occur two to five times each year.

Light from the Sun

1. **✓ Checkpoint** How is a total lunar eclipse different from other lunar eclipses?
2. **Health** in Science Why should you never look directly at the Sun?

Viewing a Solar Eclipse Safely

NEVER look directly at the Sun, even during an eclipse. Looking through binoculars, sunglasses, smoked glass, exposed film, or a telescope does not protect your eyes. Using any of them to watch the Sun, even for a very short time, could cause permanent damage to your eyes, including blindness.

To view a solar eclipse safely, view its image on a screen. Sit or stand with your back to the Sun. Punch or cut a small hole, up to 2 mm across, in a sheet of paper or cardboard. Hold it up in front of you. Place a second piece of paper or cardboard behind the first sheet. As sunlight passes over your shoulder and through the hole in the first sheet, you can see an image of the eclipse on the second sheet. Try it out before the eclipse starts so you know how to place the paper. The eclipse will not last long.

Stars

Scientists estimate that there may be 1,000,000,000,000,000,000,000 stars in the known universe. That's 1 billion trillion, or 1 followed by 21 zeroes! The Sun is the star that is nearest Earth and is most important for us. It provides energy and light to living things on Earth.

Like all stars, the Sun is a hot ball of gas. It is an ordinary star. Many stars are much bigger, brighter, or hotter than the Sun. Many more are smaller, dimmer, and cooler.

During the day, you cannot see stars because the Sun is so bright. Even at night, if you are in a city that has many lights, or if the sky is not clear, you may be able to see only a few of the brightest stars. The light from stars that are very far away appears faint when it reaches Earth. The stars look like tiny dots of light. Many stars in the sky are so faint or far away that you cannot see them at all with only your eyes. But you could see some of them through a telescope.

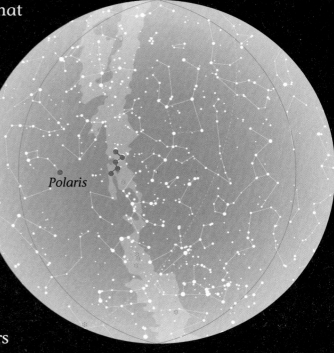

During late fall and winter in the Northern Hemisphere, Cassiopeia is almost directly overhead.

Polaris

Star Patterns

For thousands of years, people have noticed that the stars appear in shapes and patterns in the sky. These star patterns are called **constellations.** Astronomers divide the sky into 88 constellations. People often identify the stars by the constellations they are part of. The constellations are very far away from us. The stars that we see in each constellation appear to be close to each other. Actually, they may be very far apart in space.

As Earth rotates around its axis, stars appear to move across the sky. At the equator, the stars seem to move in straight lines. They rise in the east and set in the west every 24 hours. If you are near one of the poles, the stars appear to rotate in a circle in the sky. People in the Southern Hemisphere don't see the same constellations as people in the Northern Hemisphere.

In the Northern Hemisphere, the North Star, or Polaris, appears in the sky above the North Pole. Earth rotates around its axis, and the North Pole is at the northern end of the axis. Polaris does not seem to move in the sky. The stars near it do not rise or set. They seem to rotate around Polaris. These stars are in the constellations Ursa Major (the Great Bear), Ursa Minor (the Little Bear), Cepheus (the King), Cassiopeia (the Queen), and Draco (the Dragon).

Seven stars in the constellation Ursa Major make up the Big Dipper. The two stars that form the end of the dipper's bowl can help you find Polaris. Look at the pictures to see how the positions of the constellations change during the year.

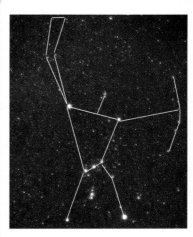

Orion

During the winter in the Northern Hemisphere, that bright constellation you see in the southern sky is Orion, the Hunter. Orion has 7 bright stars, more than any other constellation. Three stars in a line form his belt. To find Orion in the sky, look for these 3 stars. Then trace up to his shoulder. The bright star there is named Betelgeuse. It is about 400 times larger than the Sun and much brighter too. But it is also much farther from Earth. Rigel, the bright star in Orion's foot is also much larger, brighter, and farther from Earth than the Sun is. In March, the stars in Orion drop too low in the sky for you to see.

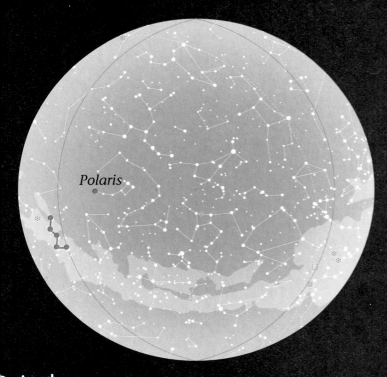

Polaris

During the summer, Cassiopeia appears much lower in the sky.

✓ **Lesson Checkpoint**

1. Why does the Moon remain partly visible during a lunar eclipse?
2. Why do distant stars that are actually very far from each other appear to be close together in the sky?
3. 🔄 **Cause and Effect** What kinds of motion cause solar and lunar eclipses? Explain.

Investigate How can you make a star finder?

Materials

Star Finder Pattern

Star Wheel

folder

scissors and glue

stapler

What to Do

1 Glue the Star Finder Pattern on a folder.

Place the edge of the Star Finder along the folded edge of the file folder, as shown.

After gluing, cut out the oval.

2 Close the folder. Cut out the star finder.

Cut along the edge of the Star Finder.

Do not cut the folded edge of the file folder.

Staple the front of the folder to the back.

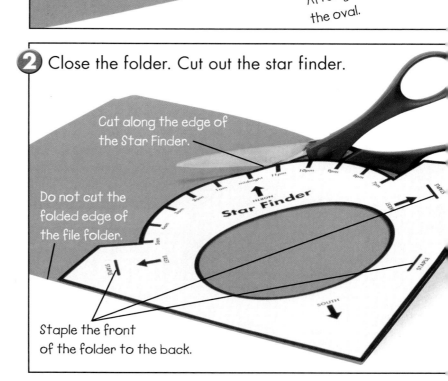

Process Skills

You **observe** when you gather information using your eyes.

3 Cut out the Star Wheel. Slide it into the Star Finder.

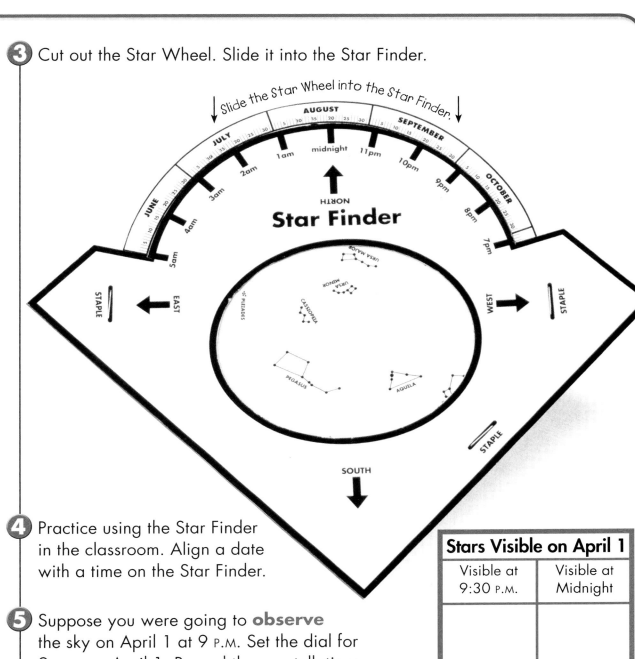

Slide the Star Wheel into the Star Finder.

Star Finder

4 Practice using the Star Finder in the classroom. Align a date with a time on the Star Finder.

5 Suppose you were going to **observe** the sky on April 1 at 9 P.M. Set the dial for 9 P.M. on April 1. Record the constellations you could see. Now set the dial for midnight. Record the constellations you could see.

Explain Your Results

Which constellations could you **observe** at 9 P.M. that are not visible at midnight? Explain why.

Stars Visible on April 1	
Visible at 9:30 P.M.	Visible at Midnight

Go Further

Do all stars have the same brightness, size, and color? How do stars appear to move daily and seasonally? If possible in your area, use your star finder to help find out. Also, look for star patterns, such as the Big Dipper.

Math in Science

Comparing Hours of Daylight

In the Northern and Southern Hemispheres, the number of hours of daylight changes with the seasons. At the equator, this number does not change very much. The table below shows the average number of daylight hours for each month in three cities.

Average Number of Daylight Hours			
Month	Chicago, IL	Quito, Ecuador	Rio de Janeiro, Brazil
January	9.5	12.1	13.4
February	10.6	12.1	12.9
March	12.0	12.1	12.2
April	13.4	12.1	11.6
May	14.6	12.1	11.0
June	15.2	12.1	10.8
July	14.9	12.1	10.9
August	13.8	12.1	11.4
September	12.5	12.1	12.0
October	11.0	12.1	12.6
November	9.8	12.1	13.2
December	9.2	12.1	13.5

Chicago

Equator

Quito

Rio de Janeiro

Use the data in the table to answer the questions.

1. Find the average number (mean) hours of daylight in Chicago for October, November, and December.

2. In June, how many more hours of daylight are there in Chicago than in Rio de Janeiro?

3. Notice the pattern in the data for each of the three cities. How are the patterns different?

4. In which month is the data for the three cities the most alike?

Lab zone Take-Home Activity

Find data about the average number of daylight hours for each month in your area. Compare these data with the data for Chicago. Write a paragraph about why the data are similar or different.

Use Vocabulary

axis (p. 496)	**orbit** (p. 498)
constellation (p. 504)	**revolution** (p. 498)
eclipse (p. 502)	**rotation** (p. 496)
ellipse (p. 498)	**solar eclipse** (p. 503)
lunar eclipse (p. 502)	

Use the term from the list above that best completes the sentence.

1. Earth spins around its _____.

2. Earth completes one _____ each day.

3. A(n) _____ is part of the sky used to identify stars.

4. Earth's path around the Sun is its _____ .

5. During a(n) _____, the Moon casts its shadow on Earth.

6. During a(n) _____, the Moon passes through Earth's shadow.

7. Earth takes a year to complete one _____ around the Sun.

8. A(n) _____ occurs when an object in space gets between the Sun and another object.

9. Earth's path around the Sun is shaped like a(n) _____.

Explain Concepts

10. Explain how and why shadows change during the day.

11. Explain why you always see the same side of the Moon.

Process Skills

12. **Infer** The graph shows daylight hours in Miami, Florida (red bars) and Boston, Massachusetts (blue bars). Where do the daylight hours vary more? Explain why this is so.

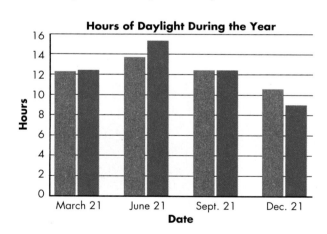

Hours of Daylight During the Year

13. **Form a hypothesis** Some stars are much bigger and brighter than the Sun. Why does the light that we see from these stars look very faint?

14. **Predict** Suppose you have located where Earth is today on a map showing the Sun and all of the planets. Where will Earth be in six months?

 Cause and Effect

15. Explain what causes seasonal changes. Use a graphic organizer and the ideas below to help.

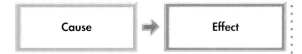

| Cause | → | Effect |

- Earth revolves around the Sun.
- Earth's axis is tilted.
- Sun's path in the sky changes.
- Sunlight is more direct or less direct.
- Hours of sunlight vary.
- Temperatures vary.

 ## Test Prep

Choose the letter that best completes the statement.

16. The Sun rises in the east and sets in the west because
- Ⓐ it depends on which hemisphere you are in.
- Ⓑ the Sun moves in the same direction as the Moon.
- Ⓒ Earth rotates from east to west.
- Ⓓ Earth rotates from west to east.

17. One reason seasons change on Earth is that
- Ⓕ the Sun's gravity is very strong.
- Ⓖ Earth's axis is tilted.
- Ⓗ the Moon revolves around Earth.
- Ⓘ Earth rotates around its own axis.

18. The constellations seen in the Northern Hemisphere that never appear to rise or completely set are
- Ⓐ near Polaris.
- Ⓑ in Ursa Major.
- Ⓒ near the edge of the visible sky.
- Ⓓ the largest ones.

19. Explain why the answer you selected for Question 18 is best. For each answer you did not select, give a reason why it is not the best choice.

20. Writing in Science **Expository**
Earth spins on its axis and orbits the Sun. Yet, to us, Earth doesn't seem to move. Write a paragraph that explains this to a younger child.

Robert B. Lee III

Robert B. Lee III
is a NASA
research scientist.

Robert B. Lee III grew up in Norfolk, Virginia. Like three of his seven brothers and sisters, young Robert had a job. When he was 11 years old, he began a 10-mile paper route. As he collected payment from his customers, he learned to make change quickly with the money he had. This combined two things he enjoyed, problem solving and mathematics.

He made toy airplanes from reeds and other materials that grew in swampy areas near his home. Airplanes fascinated him. He liked the challenge of making his airplanes fly better. Robert was in junior high school when the United States launched its first rocket. His project for metal-working class was a model rocket.

Robert participated in various sports and in math and science competitions in high school. As part of a training program at Norfolk State College, he began working at NASA's Langley Research Center in Hampton, VA. After he graduated from college, he became a staff scientist at Langley.

Much of Mr. Lee's research focuses on remote sensing. This means using instruments on Earth or in satellites to take measurements of the Sun, Earth's upper atmosphere, and atmospheres of other planets. Mr. Lee and his team compare data provided by projects such as CERES and ERBE to learn about the Sun's radiation. The data show changes in the brightness of the Sun, the causes of the changes, and how the changes may affect Earth's climate.

Robert B. Lee III travels to other countries to share the results of his research. But he still does most of his problem solving close to his boyhood home.

Lab zone Take-Home Activity

As part of his research, Mr. Lee is tracking sunspots. Use the Internet or other sources to find information about sunspots. Write a paragraph in your **science journal** to summarize what you learn.

EC NTL 10 9 8 7 6 5 4 3

You Will Discover

○ what makes up our solar system.

○ the characteristics of the planets.

○ what keeps planets and moons in motion.

Chapter 18

Inner and Outer Planets

Discovery Channel School
Student DVD

online
Student Edition
sfsuccessnet.com

How is Earth different from other planets in our solar system?

galaxy

universe

astronomy

craters

Chapter 18 Vocabulary

universe page 519

galaxy page 519

astronomy page 519

solar system page 520

craters page 522

space probe page 522

satellite page 524

solar system

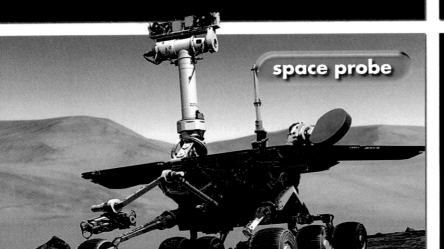

space probe

satellite

Lab zone Directed Inquiry

Explore How can you compare the sizes of planets?

Materials

Planet Patterns 1 and
Planet Patterns 2

scissors

metric ruler

Process Skills

You identified the paper "planets" by **measuring** them. The paper **models** are about 1 billionth of the diameter of the real planets. The paper planets are scale models.

What to Do

1 **Measure** the diameter of each paper "planet." Then use your measurements and chart to find each planet's name. Label each planet. Cut out each planet.

2 Use the cutouts as **models** of the planets. Put them in order by size. Compare the sizes of the planets.

Name of Planet	Diameter of Planet (nearest 100 km)	Diameter of Model (mm)	Average Distance from Sun (nearest 100,000 km)
Mercury (Label it *M*.)	4,900 km	5 mm	57,900,000 km
Venus	12,100 km	12 mm	108,200,000 km
Earth	12,800 km	13 mm	149,600,000 km
Mars	6,800 km	7 mm	227,900,000 km
Jupiter	143,000 km	143 mm	778,400,000 km
Saturn	120,500 km	121 mm	1,426,700,000 km
Uranus	51,000 km	51 mm	2,871,000,000 km
Neptune	49,500 km	50 mm	4,498,300,000 km
Pluto (Label it *P*.)	2,300 km	2 mm	5,906,300,000 km

3 Put the planets in order by distance from the Sun.

Explain Your Results

1. Explain how **measuring** helped you identify each paper **model**.

2. Compare the sizes of Earth, Venus, and Jupiter.

3. How many planets are smaller than Earth? larger than Earth?

How to Read Science

Predicting

A **prediction** is a statement about what you think will happen in the future. To make a prediction, you think of what you have learned in the past. You can also use observations and **measurements** to look for patterns that suggest what to expect in the future.

The information in an old newspaper article gives clues to future events.

Newpaper Article

Comet to Return!

March 5, 1986 Edmund Halley studied the laws of motion and data from comets. He noticed that a comet visible in 1682 followed the same long, narrow path as comets in 1607 and 1531. He said that all three were really the same comet. In 1705, he predicted that the comet would return in 1759. His prediction came true 17 years after he died. The comet was named in his honor. Halley's Comet appeared in 1835 and 1910. Now in 1986, it will pass close to Earth again.

Apply It!

Use what you know and the information from the article to **predict** the next time Halley's Comet will pass close to Earth.

Information

Prediction

You Are There!

On a clear night you gaze up at the sky. You see thousands and thousands of stars. Some are brighter than others. You notice a cloudy band that stretches across the sky. You are seeing part of the Milky Way, our home galaxy. The Milky Way has so many stars that you could not count them in a lifetime. We cannot see our galaxy as a whole, but scientists can see other galaxies that they think are similar to ours. Cameras sent into space years ago have only recently left the very small part of our galaxy that we call home, the solar system. What did these cameras pass on their journey?

Lesson 1

What makes up the universe?

Planets in our solar system travel around the Sun. Earth is a small part of the solar system. The solar system is only a small part of a vast universe.

The Universe and the Milky Way

You know your home address, but do you know your address in the **universe**? The universe is all of space and everything in it. Most of the universe is empty space.

The universe has millions of galaxies. A **galaxy** is a system of dust, gas, and many millions of stars held together by gravity. We live in the Milky Way galaxy. The Milky Way is shaped like a flat spiral. Other galaxies have different shapes. Our Sun is located near the edge of our galaxy. It is one of billions of stars in the Milky Way.

People have always watched objects move across the sky. The study of the Sun, Moon, stars, and other objects in space is **astronomy**. Experts think that the Great Pyramids in ancient Egypt were built to line up with the stars.

The Egyptians were not the only ones who used principles of astronomy. Greeks, Chinese, Indians, Arabs, and other early civilizations all used astronomy to decide when they should plant or harvest crops. Sailors on the open sea did not have landmarks to tell them where they were. They used the Sun and the stars.

1. ✓Checkpoint Describe what makes up the universe.
2. Social Studies in Science Use the Internet or other sources to find how early civilizations used the positions of certain stars for such buildings as Mayan pyramids and Greek temples. Draw a picture that shows what you learned.

Our Solar System

The solar system includes the Sun, the planets, their moons, and other objects. Everything in the solar system revolves around the Sun. That is, each object moves in a path, or orbit, around the Sun. A planet is a very large, ball-shaped object that moves around a star, such as the Sun. Planets are cooler and smaller than stars. They don't give off their own visible light, either. They may seem to shine because they reflect the light from the star they orbit.

Our solar system has inner and outer planets. The inner planets are Mercury, Venus, Earth, and Mars. The outer planets are Jupiter, Saturn, Uranus, Neptune, and Pluto. An area called the asteroid belt is between the inner planets and outer planets. Asteroids are rocky objects that also orbit the Sun but are too small to be called planets. As you probably inferred, the asteroid belt is a part of the solar system that has many asteroids.

The sizes and distances in this diagram are not true to scale. Also, the planets rarely line up.

Asteroid belt

Jupiter

Saturn

Earth

Venus

Mercury

Mars

Uranus

When they observe the Sun, scientists use special telescopes with special cameras. They use special filters to photograph and record radiation from the Sun. Looking at the Sun can damage your eyes. You should never look directly at the Sun or use an ordinary telelscope to observe the Sun.

Gravity is the force that keeps Earth and other objects in their orbits. Planets tend to move in a straight line. But the force of gravity affects the motion of the planets. Because the Sun is so massive, its gravity pulls the planets toward it. As a result, the planets move in curved paths around the Sun. The force of gravity between each planet and the Sun keeps even the outer planets in their orbits. The orbits are elliptical. That is, they are slightly flattened circles. The orbits of planets closest to the Sun are almost circular. The orbits of the outer planets are longer and narrower.

Astronomers have discovered other planets in orbit around other stars. So, it is possible that there are other solar systems besides ours.

The Sun

Our Sun is a medium sized star. It is the largest body in the solar system. Like all stars, the Sun is a huge ball of hot, glowing gases. Energy from the Sun provides light and heats Earth. The outer parts of the Sun are much cooler than the inner parts. Scientists estimate that the outer part of the Sun is about 5,500°C (10,000°F). They think that the inner core is as hot as 15,000,000°C!

Like Earth, the Sun has a magnetic field. The Sun's magnetic field can become very strong in some places. Large loops of gas can extend from the Sun's surface in these areas. Dark spots called sunspots also appear at places where the magnetic field is very strong.

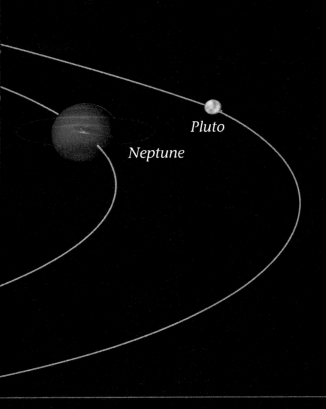

Pluto

Neptune

✓ Lesson Checkpoint

1. Why do planets orbit around the Sun?
2. Name three different types of objects in our solar system.
3. **Writing in Science** **Descriptive** In your **science journal,** describe the characteristics of the Sun.

Lesson 2

What are the inner planets?

The four planets closest to the Sun are known as the inner planets. Mercury, Venus, Earth, and Mars are all small rocky planets.

This picture of Mercury was made by joining many smaller photos that were taken by *Mariner 10*. No photos were taken of the area that looks smooth.

Mercury

Mercury is the planet closest to the Sun. It is a small planet, a little bigger than Earth's moon. Mercury is covered with thousands of dents. The dents are shaped like bowls and are called **craters.** Craters were made when meteorites crashed into Mercury's surface long ago. A meteorite is a rock from space that has struck the surface of a planet or a moon.

In 1974 scientists sent the *Mariner 10* space probe to visit Mercury. A **space probe** is a vehicle that carries cameras and other tools for studying different objects in space.

Mercury Facts

Average distance from Sun
57,900,000 km (35,983,000 mi)

Diameter
4,879 km (3,032 mi)

Length of day as measured in Earth time
59 days

Length of year as measured in Earth time
88 days

Average surface temperature
117°C (243°F)

Moons
none

Weight of a person who is 100 lb on Earth
38 lb

Too Hot and Too Cold

Mercury has almost no atmosphere. Because it is so close to the Sun, Mercury is scorching hot during the day. Daytime temperatures are four or five times greater than the hottest place on Earth. But with no atmosphere to hold in the heat, Mercury is very cold at night.

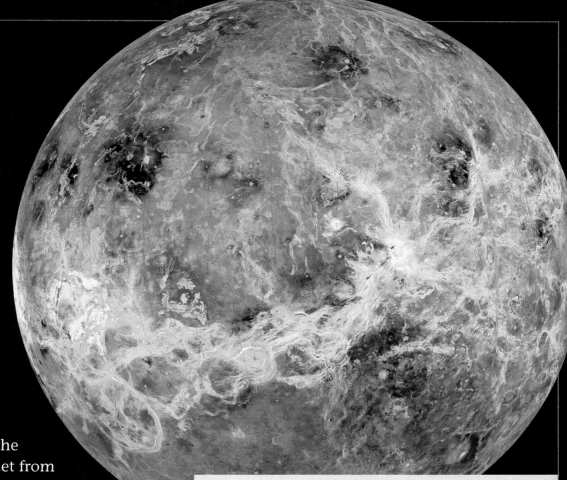

Venus

Venus is the
second planet from
the Sun. It is about
the same size as Earth,
but Venus turns in the
opposite direction.

Like Mercury, Venus is very
hot and dry. Unlike Mercury,
Venus has an atmosphere made
of thick, swirling clouds. The
clouds of Venus are burning hot
and poisonous! There are strong
winds and lightning. The clouds
also are good at reflecting the
Sun's light. This makes Venus one
of the brightest objects in Earth's
night sky.

Venus Facts

Average distance from Sun
108,200,000 km (67,200,000 mi)

Diameter
12,104 km (7,521 mi)

Length of day as measured in Earth time
243 days (spins backward)

Length of year as measured in Earth time
225 days

Average surface temperature
464°C (867°F)

Moons
none

Weight of a person who is 100 lb on Earth
91 lb

1. **✓Checkpoint** What are some reasons why people cannot live on Mercury or Venus?
2. **Math** in Science How much farther from the Sun is Venus than is Mercury?

Earth

Earth, our home, is the third planet from the Sun. It is also the solar system's largest rocky planet. Earth is the only planet that has liquid water on its surface. In fact, most of Earth's surface is covered with water.

Earth is wrapped in a layer of gas that is about 150 kilometers (93 miles) thick. This layer of gas, or atmosphere, makes life possible on Earth. It filters out some of the Sun's harmful rays. It also contains nitrogen, oxygen, carbon dioxide, and water vapor. Plants and animals on Earth use these gases. Earth is the only planet in the solar system known to support life.

Earth Facts

Average distance from Sun
149,600,000 km (93,000,000 mi)

Diameter
12,756 km (7,926 mi)

Length of day as measured in Earth time
24 hours

Length of year as measured in Earth time
365 days

Average surface temperature
15°C (59°F)

Moons
1

Weight of a person who is 100 lb on Earth
100 lb

The Moon

Moons are satellites of planets. A satellite is an object that orbits another object in space. Just as planets revolve around the Sun because of gravity, moons revolve around planets. The force of gravity between a planet and its moons keeps the moons in their orbits.

Earth has one large moon. The Moon is about one-fourth the size of Earth. The Moon has no atmosphere. It has many craters that formed when meteorites crashed onto its surface.

Exploring the Moon

Space exploration started in 1957 when the former Soviet Union launched *Sputnik*, the first artificial satellite. The Soviet Union sent the first space probes to the Moon in 1959. These spacecraft did not carry people.

In 1961, Yuri Gagarin, a Soviet cosmonaut, became the first person to travel in space. His journey on *Vostok I* circled Earth in less than 2 hours. In 1969, Americans Neil Armstrong and Buzz Aldrin were the first people to step onto the powdery soil that covers the Moon's surface. The Moon has no atmosphere to create wind or rain, so their footprints will remain for years to come.

1. ✓**Checkpoint** What makes life possible on Earth?
2. **Writing** in Science **Narrative** In your **science journal,** write what you think it would be like to live on the Moon.

Mars

The fourth planet from the Sun is Mars. The rocks and soil that cover much of Mars contain the mineral iron oxide. This mineral is reddish-brown in color. It is the same material that makes up rust. This has given Mars its nickname, the "Red Planet." Mars has two deeply cratered moons. Phobos, one of the moons, is very close to Mars. It is closer to Mars than any other moon is to any other planet.

Mars Facts

Average distance from Sun
227,900,000 km (141,600,000 mi)

Diameter
6,794 km (4,222 mi)

Length of day as measured in Earth time
24.6 hours

Length of year as measured in Earth time
687 days

Average surface temperature
−63°C (−81°F)

Moons
2

Weight of a person who is 100 lb on Earth
38 lb

The atmosphere on Mars does not have enough oxygen to support complex life forms such as plants and animals. Winds on Mars cause dust storms. The dust storms are sometimes so large that they cover the entire planet.

Mars has polar caps that grow in the Martian winter and shrink in the summer. Mars has many volcanoes. It also has a canyon that's bigger than Earth's Grand Canyon. This canyon, the Valles Marineris, is more than 4,000 kilometers long. Earth's Grand Canyon in Arizona is 446 kilometers long.

About $\frac{2}{3}$ of the surface of Mars is dry and is covered by dust and rocks.

Several probes have successfully landed on Mars. The first one, *Viking I*, touched down on Mars in 1976. As part of the Pathfinder mission in 1997, a 30-cm tall box-shaped robot explored part of Mars. The robot was named *Sojourner*. Then, in January 2004, the twin robot Mars Exploration Rovers *Spirit* and *Opportunity*, landed. *Spirit* and *Opportunity* gathered data and sent them back to Earth. Scientists hope the data will provide much information about materials that make up Mars. They hope some of the data will provide evidence that Mars has or once had water.

✓ **Lesson Checkpoint**

1. Why is the soil on Mars red?
2. What characteristics do Earth and Mars have in common?
3. **Predict** What might scientists predict if the rovers find water on Mars?

What do we know about Jupiter, Saturn, and Uranus?

Jupiter, Saturn, and Uranus are outer planets. Their orbits are beyond the asteroid belt. All three planets are gas giants with many moons.

Jupiter

Jupiter, the fifth planet from the Sun, is a gas giant. A gas giant is a very large planet made mostly of gases. Jupiter's atmosphere is mainly hydrogen and helium. Jupiter is the largest planet in our solar system. In fact, if it were hollow, it is so big that all of the other planets could fit inside it!

Jupiter Facts

Average Distance from Sun
778,400,000 km (484,000,000 mi)

Diameter
142,984 km (88,846 mi)

Length of day as measured in Earth time
10 hours

Length of year as measured in Earth time
12 years

Average surface temperature
–148°C (–234°F)

Moons
at least 63

Rings
yes

Weight of a person who is 100 lb on Earth
214 lb

Jupiter's atmosphere has a weather system called the Great Red Spot that has been raging for centuries. It is a disturbance that is more than three times the size of Earth.

Jupiter's bands of clouds make it one of the most colorful objects in the solar system.

Jupiter's Moons

Jupiter has many moons. Galileo was the first person to see the four largest moons through his telescope in 1610. They are about the size of Earth's moon. Jupiter also has rings, but they are too dark to be seen from Earth.

Io has more active volcanoes than any other body in the solar system. The volcanoes give off sulfur. The sulfur shows up as yellows, oranges, and greenish yellows. Io is the solar system's most colorful moon.

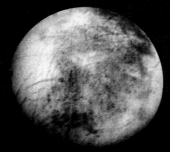

Europa is the smoothest object in the solar system. Its crust is frozen, but a liquid ocean might lie beneath the crust. Some scientists believe there may be living organisms on Europa.

Ganymede is the largest moon in the solar system. It is bigger than Mercury and Pluto. Ice covers one third of its surface. It may even have a saltwater ocean!

Callisto is more heavily cratered than any other object in the solar system. The impacts of meteorites have left large cracks in its surface. Scientists think Callisto has a frozen ocean beneath its crust.

1. ✔ Checkpoint   What is a gas giant?
2. Art in Science   Draw a picture of what you think the surface of one of Jupiter's moons would look like.

529

Saturn

The sixth planet from the Sun, Saturn is also a gas giant. Like Jupiter, Saturn's atmosphere is mostly hydrogen and helium. Saturn is very large, but it has only a small amount of matter.

The *Voyager* space probe explored Saturn's rings. It showed that the particles that make up the rings range in size from tiny grains to boulders. They are probably made of ice, dust, and chunks of rock.

Galileo's Handles

When Galileo saw Saturn through his telescope, he was surprised. He saw what looked like a planet with handles! The "handles" were actually the brilliant ring system that orbits the planet.

Galileo Galilei lived from 1564 to 1642. He was a mathematician and astronomer. He agreed with Copernicus that all planets revolve around the Sun. Galileo used a telescope to observe the Sun, Moon, planets, and stars.

Saturn Facts

Average distance from Sun
1,426,700,000 km (885,900,000 mi)

Diameter
120,536 km (74,897 mi)

Length of day as measured in Earth time
11 hours

Length of year as measured in Earth time
29.4 years

Average surface temperature
−178°C (−288°F)

Moons
at least 36

Rings
yes

Weight of a person who is 100 lb on Earth
74 lb

The thousand bright rings around Saturn are its most amazing feature.

Moons of Saturn

Saturn has many moons. Like Jupiter's moons, most of Saturn's moons are small. Its largest moon, Titan, may be the most unusual moon in the solar system. It has an atmosphere! And, Titan is larger than both Mercury and Pluto.

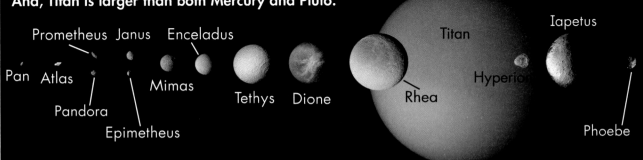

Pan Atlas Prometheus Janus Enceladus Mimas Tethys Dione Rhea Titan Hyperion Iapetus Phoebe
Pandora Epimetheus

1. **✓ Checkpoint** What are Saturn's rings made of?
2. **Writing in Science** **Expository** Research the life of Galileo. Write what you learn in your **science journal.**

531

Uranus

In 1781, William Herschel discovered a seventh planet orbiting the Sun. The gas giant Uranus is the farthest planet you can see without a telescope. Its atmosphere is hydrogen, helium, and methane. Uranus is so cold that the methane is a liquid. Tiny drops of liquid methane form a thin cloud that covers the planet. This gives Uranus its fuzzy blue-green look. Like the other gas giants, Uranus also has a ring system and many moons. But, unlike Saturn's bright ring system, the rings of Uranus are dark and hard to see with Earth-based telescopes. A space probe discovered the rings in 1977.

Rolling Through Space

Uranus rotates on its side. No one knows for sure why Uranus has this odd tilt. Scientists think that a very large object may have collided with the planet when the solar system was still forming. This bump may have knocked Uranus onto its side.

Uranus Facts

Average distance from Sun
2,871,000,000 km (1,784,000,000 mi)

Diameter
51,118 km (31,763 mi)

Length of day as measured in Earth time
17 hours (spins backward)

Length of year as measured in Earth time
84 years

Average surface temperature
–216°C (–357°F)

Moons
at least 27

Rings
yes

Weight of a person who is 100 lb on Earth
86 lb

Uranus is a gas giant with a large liquid core.

The Moons of Uranus

Today we know the planet has at least 27 moons, and more may yet be discovered. The moons farthest from Uranus are hard to see using telescopes on Earth. The moons closer to the planet were first seen with telescopes during the 1700s. They are larger moons with deep valleys, craters, and steep ridges.

Oberon

Titania

Umbriel

Ariel

Miranda

✓ Lesson Checkpoint

1. How is the atmosphere of Uranus different from that of Saturn?
2. How is Uranus different from other gas giants?
3. **Math** in Science How many years passed between the discoveries of Uranus and its ring system?

What do we know about Neptune, Pluto, and beyond?

Neptune's atmosphere is similar to that of Uranus. Like Uranus, the gas methane gives Neptune a blue color. Neptune has bands of clouds and storms similar to those on Jupiter.

Neptune is a gas giant. Pluto, however, is not a giant. In fact, it is the smallest planet in our solar system. Scientists are discovering more objects beyond Pluto.

Neptune

Neptune is the eighth planet from the Sun. It is the smallest of the gas giants. Even so, if Neptune were hollow, it could hold about 60 Earths. It is so far away that it can't be seen without a telescope. In 1846 astronomers discovered Neptune. A few days later they spotted Triton, Neptune's largest moon.

Because Neptune is so far from the Sun, its orbit is very long. Neptune takes more than 100 Earth years to orbit the Sun. It is a very windy planet. Its powerful winds blow huge storms across the planet.

A hurricane-like storm called the Great Dark Spot was tracked by the *Voyager 2* space probe in 1989.

Neptune Facts	
Average distance from Sun 4,498,300,000 km (2,795,000,000 mi)	
Diameter 49,528 km (30,775 mi)	
Length of day as measured in Earth time 16 hours	
Length of year as measured in Earth time 165 years	
Average surface temperature –214°C (–353°F)	
Moons at least 13	
Rings yes	
Weight of a person who is 100 lb on Earth 110 lb	

How Neptune Was Discovered

British astronomer John Couch Adams studied planets and other objects in space. He noticed that Uranus was not orbiting the way that he calculated it should. He concluded that the force of gravity between Uranus and another planet was affecting the orbit. A mathematician named Urbain Leverrier made calculations of his own. He used these data to predict the position and size of the proposed planet. He shared his findings with astronomers. On September 23, 1846, Johann Galle aimed his telescope where the predictions suggested he should look. He saw Neptune!

The Moons of Neptune

Neptune has at least 13 moons. The largest, Triton, is one of the coldest bodies in our solar system. Its surface temperature is about –235°C.

Astronomers think that Triton didn't form with Neptune. Instead, they think it formed farther from the Sun and was captured by Neptune's gravity.

1. ✓Checkpoint How does Neptune compare in size with other planets?
2. Math in Science How much colder is the average temperature on Triton than on Neptune?

Triton

Neptune

Neptune's rings are made of rocks and dust.

Pluto

In 1930, Clyde Tombaugh discovered a ninth planet, Pluto. It is the only outer planet that is not a gas giant. It has an icy, solid surface. Pluto is the smallest planet in the solar system. It is even smaller than Earth's moon!

Pluto's moon Charon is slightly smaller than Pluto. Charon is very close to Pluto. Many astronomers consider Pluto and Charon a double planet system since they are so close together and similar in size. Also, astronomers think the two share the same atmosphere when they are closest to the Sun.

Pluto

Charon

Pluto Facts

Average distance from Sun
5,906,300,000 km (3,670,000,000 mi)

Diameter
2,302 km (1,430 mi)

Length of day as measured in Earth time
6 days (spins backward)

Length of year as measured in Earth time
248 years

Average surface temperature
−233°C (−387°F)

Moons
at least 1

Weight of a person who is 100 lb on Earth
8 lb

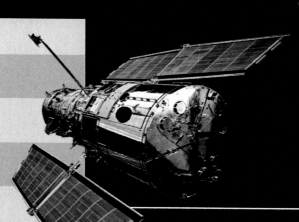

NASA's Hubble Space Telescope looked more than 3 billion miles into space and captured this image of the small, icy Pluto.

Charon

Pluto

An Odd Orbit

Pluto has an odd orbit. The other planets travel around the Sun at the same angle, while Pluto's orbit is tilted. During parts of its orbit, it is closer to the Sun than Neptune is. This occurred from 1979 to 1999. The next time this will occur is in 2237.

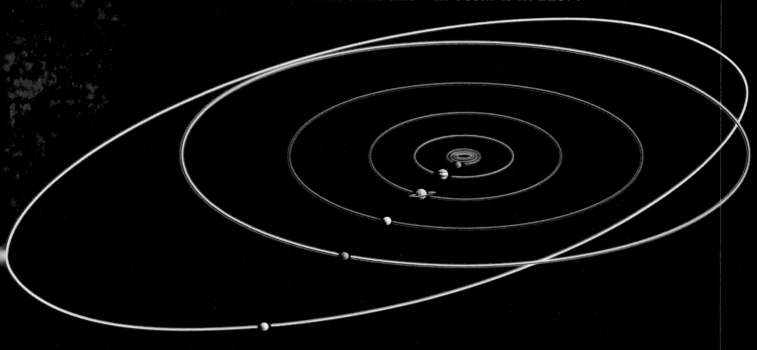

Objects Beyond Pluto

In 2003, astronomers saw a red object more than 80 billion miles from the Sun. It was the largest body discovered in the solar system since 1930. The object was named Sedna. It is smaller than Earth's moon. Its temperature is a chilly –240°C.

In 2005, scientists announced that they had found an object that is a little larger than Pluto and at least three times farther from the Sun. It has at least one moon. Until this object is named, it is called 2003 UB313.

Sedna

Pluto

The approximate size of Sedna compared to Pluto

✓ Lesson Checkpoint

1. List the planets in order from smallest to largest.
2. **Math** in Science At the closest point of its orbit, Pluto is 4,436,820,000 km from the Sun. At the farthest point, Pluto is 7,375,930,000 km from the Sun. How much farther is this?
3. ↻ Predict Will astronomers find evidence of life on Sedna?

Investigate How does spinning affect a planet's shape?

Materials

large construction paper

metric ruler

scissors

stapler

hole punch

dull pencil

Process Skills

Although a **model** is different from the real thing it represents, it can be used to learn about the real thing. By constructing, operating, and analyzing your model, you learned how spinning might affect a planet's shape.

What to Do

1 Cut 2 strips of construction paper. Cross the strips at their centers. Staple as shown.

Each strip should measure about 2.5 cm × 46 cm.

2 Bring the 4 ends together and overlap them. Staple them as shown to form a sphere.

3 Use the punch to make a hole through the center of the overlapped ends.

4 Push about 5 centimeters of the pencil through the hole.

5 Hold the pencil between your palms and move your hands back and forth to make your **model** spin. Record your observations in a chart like the one below.

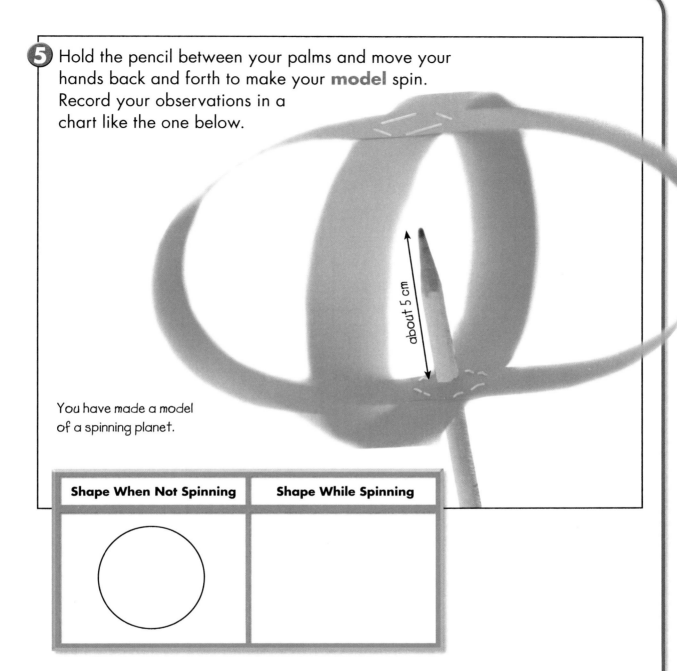

about 5 cm

You have made a model of a spinning planet.

Shape When Not Spinning	Shape While Spinning
◯	

Explain Your Results

1. Did the sphere change shape when you spun it? Make an **inference** about what happened.

2. How is your **model** similar to a spinning planet? How is it different?

Go Further

Be your own model of a spinning planet. Stand in an open area far from other students with your arms hanging loosely at your sides. Spin around twice. Feel your arms move out. Be careful not to get dizzy!

Using Data About Planets

Each planet in the solar system has the shape of a sphere. The diameter of a sphere is the distance from one point on the surface of the sphere to a point on the opposite side, passing through the center. Think of digging a tunnel that passes through the center of Earth to the opposite side. The length of that tunnel would be Earth's diameter.

The table below gives the diameter in kilometers of each planet in the solar system.

Planet	Diameter
Mercury	4,879 km
Venus	12,104 km
Earth	12,756 km
Mars	6,794 km
Jupiter	142,984 km
Saturn	120,536 km
Uranus	51,118 km
Neptune	49,528 km
Pluto	2,302 km

Copy the table on page 540. Add a third column, with the heading "Rounded Diameter."

1. Round each diameter to the nearest thousand kilometers. Write the rounded number in the table.

2. List the 9 planets with their rounded diameters in order from least to greatest. What is the median rounded diameter? Which planet has that diameter?

3. Which planet has a diameter about 10 times that of Venus?

4. Which planet has a diameter less than half that of Mercury?

Lab zone Take-Home Activity

Choose your favorite planet and do some research about it. Write a news article or a science fiction story about your planet.

Use Vocabulary

astronomy (p. 519)	**solar system** (p. 520)
craters (p. 522)	**space probe** (p. 522)
galaxy (p. 519)	
satellite (p. 524)	**universe** (p. 519)

Use the vocabulary term from the list above that completes each sentence.

1. A(n) _____ is a vehicle that carries cameras and other tools into space.

2. The study of the universe, including the Sun, Moon, stars, and planets is called _____.

3. A(n) _____ is an object that orbits another object in space.

4. Many millions of stars held together by gravity form a _____.

5. _____ are bowl-shaped holes made by meteorites.

6. The _____ is all of space and everything in it.

7. The Sun, the planets, their moons, asteroids, and other objects that revolve around the Sun make up the _____.

Explain Concepts

8. Describe the orbit of each of the planets.

9. Explain what makes Earth unique in our solar system.

10. Explain why some scientists consider Pluto to be a double planet.

11. Describe the features of the Sun that are shown in this photograph and explain what causes them.

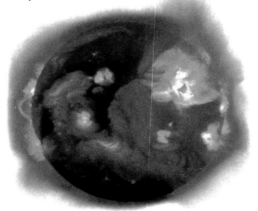

Process Skills

12. **Sequence** Order the planets from closest to farthest from the Sun.

13. **Infer** All of the gas giants have many moons. With two moons, Mars holds the record for the most moons for the smaller rocky planets. Infer why gas giants have more moons than rocky planets.

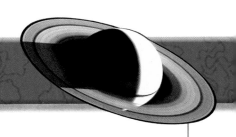

 Predicting

14. All planets in our solar system orbit the Sun. Scientists have identified more than 100 planets orbiting other stars. Suppose they discover one of these planets is similar to gas giants in the solar system. Copy and complete the graphic organizer to help predict other characteristics of this planet.

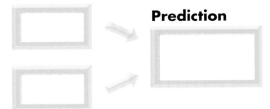

Test Prep

Choose the letter that best completes the statement or answers the question.

15. The smallest of the gas giants is
  Ⓐ Pluto.
  Ⓑ Uranus.
  Ⓒ Saturn.
  Ⓓ Neptune.

16. The object in our solar system with the strongest gravitational pull is
  Ⓕ Jupiter.
  Ⓖ the Sun.
  Ⓗ Earth.
  Ⓘ the Moon.

17. Who discovered the planet Pluto?
  Ⓐ John Couch Adams
  Ⓑ Urbain Leverrier
  Ⓒ Clyde Tombaugh
  Ⓓ Johann Galle

18. What kind of storm sometimes covers the entire planet of Mars?
  Ⓕ thunderstorm
  Ⓖ tropical storm
  Ⓗ dust storm
  Ⓘ ice storm

19. Explain why the answer you chose for Question 18 is best. For each answer you did not choose, give a reason why it is not the best choice.

20. Writing in Science **Persuasive** Astronomers have observed many moons orbiting planets. Which planet do you think is likely to have moons that astronomers have not yet discovered? Give reasons to convince others why your choice is reasonable.

Nicolaus Copernicus

Nicolaus Copernicus was born in Torun, Poland, on February 19, 1473. He attended the University of Krakow, where he studied many subjects, including astronomy.

In his astronomy classes, Copernicus learned about Ptolemy's model of the universe. Ptolemy was an astronomer in Alexandria, Egypt, around A.D. 150. Ptolemy used his observations to develop a model of the universe. According to this model, Earth was at the center of the universe. Everything else revolved around Earth. Copernicus studied the works of Ptolemy and other astronomers. Copernicus developed a different theory of how to model the universe. He said objects in space moved in different ways than those Ptolemy had described. He thought Earth moved around the Sun.

Throughout his lifetime, Copernicus carefully recorded what he observed. He also considered what others observed. In 1543, he published *On the Revolutions of Heavenly Spheres.* This book said that Earth rotates on an axis and revolves around the Sun. Copernicus listened to new ideas even though they were different from the beliefs of his time. He paved the way for modern astronomers.

Lab zone Take-Home Activity

Be a sky-watcher like Copernicus. Each night for 2 weeks, look at the sky directly overhead at sunset. Write about what you see in your **science journal.**

EC NTL 10 9 8 7 6 5 4 3

Chapter 19
Effects of Technology

You Will Discover

- how technology meets the challenges of our lives.
- how we use technology in communication and transportation.

online
Student Edition
sfsuccessnet.com

How do the devices and products of technology affect the way we live?

technology

optical fibers

communication

546

Chapter 19 Vocabulary

technology
page 551

optical fibers
page 554

communication
page 556

telecommunications
page 557

vehicle page 558

telecommunications

vehicle

Explore How do communications satellites work?

Communications satellites orbiting Earth help move signals from place to place.

Materials

large coffee can

black and white construction paper

scissors and tape

metric ruler and clay

plastic mirror and flashlight

What to Do

1 **Make a model** of a communications satellite as shown, moving a signal halfway around the Earth.

2 Place the mirror so the light from the flashlight hits the white paper.

flashlight = transmitter

can = Earth

paper = receiver

plastic mirror = communications satellite

clay   clay

Explain Your Results

Infer How do you think a communications satellite helps to send signals from place to place?

Process Skills

After you observe how light is reflected in your **model**, you can **infer** how a communications satellite works.

How to Read Science

Reading Skills

Main Idea and Details

The **main idea** is the most important idea discussed in a reading selection. It is the most important idea shown in a picture or model. As you read a selection or look at a picture take note of **details** that make the main idea clearer. Some details may explain the main idea. Other details may give examples to support the main idea.

- The main idea of a paragraph is usually found in the topic sentence. It is often the first sentence of the paragraph.

- You can use details that are familiar to you to make **inferences.**

Now read the following newspaper article.

Newspaper Article

Since it was first used on people in 1977, magnetic resonance imaging (MRI) has become a major problem-solving tool for doctors. This medical technology uses electromagnetic waves. The waves make 3-D images of the body. Doctors can find problems inside the body without cutting into it. They are able to see right through bones and tissue. They are able to diagnose injuries and diseases.

Apply It!
Copy and complete the graphic organizer to show the **main idea and details** in the newspaper article. Use the graphic organizer to help you **infer** another reason MRI technology is helpful.

Detail	Detail	Detail

Main Idea

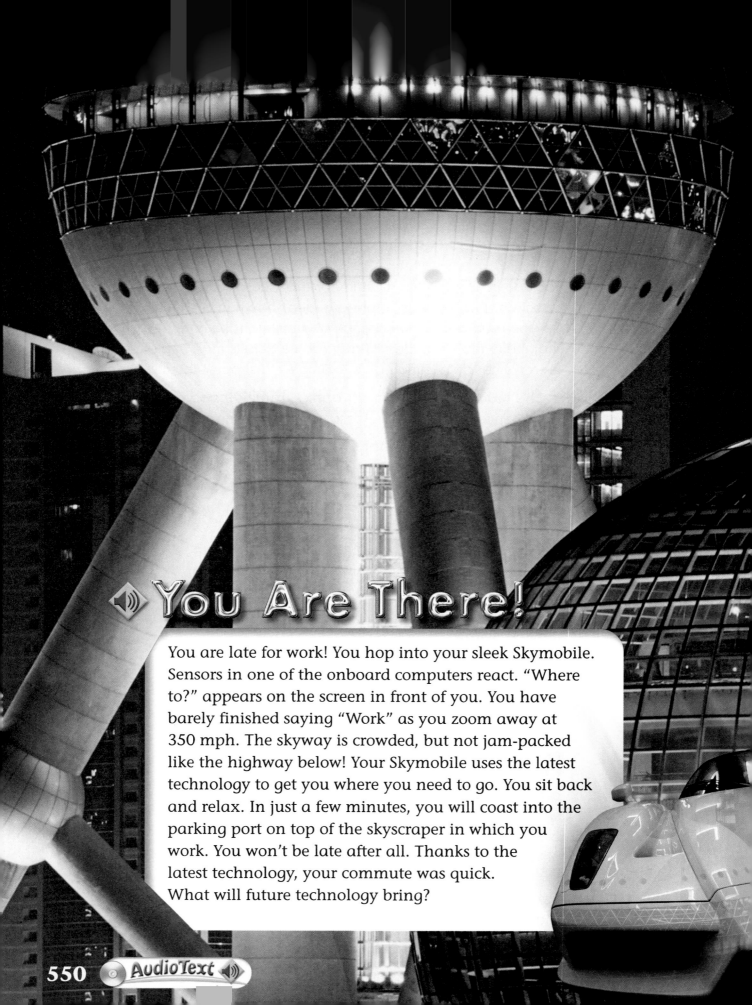

🔊 You Are There!

You are late for work! You hop into your sleek Skymobile. Sensors in one of the onboard computers react. "Where to?" appears on the screen in front of you. You have barely finished saying "Work" as you zoom away at 350 mph. The skyway is crowded, but not jam-packed like the highway below! Your Skymobile uses the latest technology to get you where you need to go. You sit back and relax. In just a few minutes, you will coast into the parking port on top of the skyscraper in which you work. You won't be late after all. Thanks to the latest technology, your commute was quick. What will future technology bring?

Lesson 1

How does technology affect our lives?

People use technology to make their lives more comfortable and productive. But using technology to solve one problem can cause a different problem.

New Challenges

You may not be zooming through the skies in your Skymobile just yet. But you are using technology, in many ways, in your own life right now. **Technology** is the knowledge, processes, and products that we use to solve problems and make our work easier. It helps us meet our needs and make our lives more comfortable, healthy, and useful.

Technology has a huge effect on people and other living things. Some developments have unintended effects. Some products of technology can hurt people, animals, and plants. Motor vehicle emissions, industrial waste, and insecticides have some bad side effects. Many countries, like the United States, face problems with air, water, soil, and noise pollution.

Most people agree that technology has helped us greatly. New technologies are always changing the ways people do their jobs. In many cases, machines now do things that people once did. And that can mean that people lose their jobs. But at the same time technology makes unexpected problems, it can solve them, too. New technologies may lead to machines that do dangerous work that was once done by people. And, new technologies lead to new jobs—many in the electronics industry.

1. **✓Checkpoint** What trouble has some technology caused in the United States and other countries?
2. **Writing** in Science **Expository** Write an informative paragraph in your **science journal** about the forms of technology you have used in the last 24 hours. Explain whether each form of technology helped make you more comfortable, productive, or healthy.

551

From Hitchhiker to Invention

Prickly with tiny hooks, the bur has been known to hitch rides on animals! This little bit of nature led to an important product that people make. An engineer was pulling burs off his clothing and from his dog's fur. He got the idea for Velcro®, a sticky fastener made of tiny hooks and loops. Velcro® is made of nylon or polyester. It is used in clothing, medical equipment, and sports gear. Maybe your shoes are fastened with it!

A close-up of Velcro®

Technology and Materials

This skater is too busy concentrating on the next move to notice all the products of technology. Materials that are not found in nature have come our way because of technology. In-line skates and gear are made from different materials such as plastic, metal, rubber, and nylon. Some of these materials are made from natural resources. But others are made from materials that people have made from natural resources.

For example, iron ore, a natural resource, is heated to make the steel for the bearings, screws, and axles. To make these parts, liquid metal is poured into different molds. Plastic is made from chemicals. Then it is shaped into shoe parts, buckles, and protective gear. The covering on knee and elbow pads and wrist guards may be made from nylon, a type of plastic. The cloth that lines the inside of the skates may be polyester. Clothing can be made from polyester too. Certain threads, such as polyester, are made by people from chemicals or recycled plastic materials. Each day technology leads to new inventions and improves old ones.

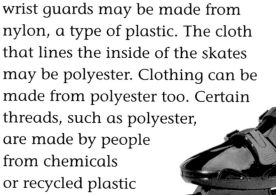

Technology Keeps Us Healthy

You know that technology helps keep us safe and healthy. It's watching out for the skater! The materials used in protective gear help lower the number of serious injuries that come with in-line skating. What happens if the skater takes a fall? The helmet will help protect the skater's head. Plastic cushions in the knee and elbow pads and in the wrist guards will also absorb some of the crash.

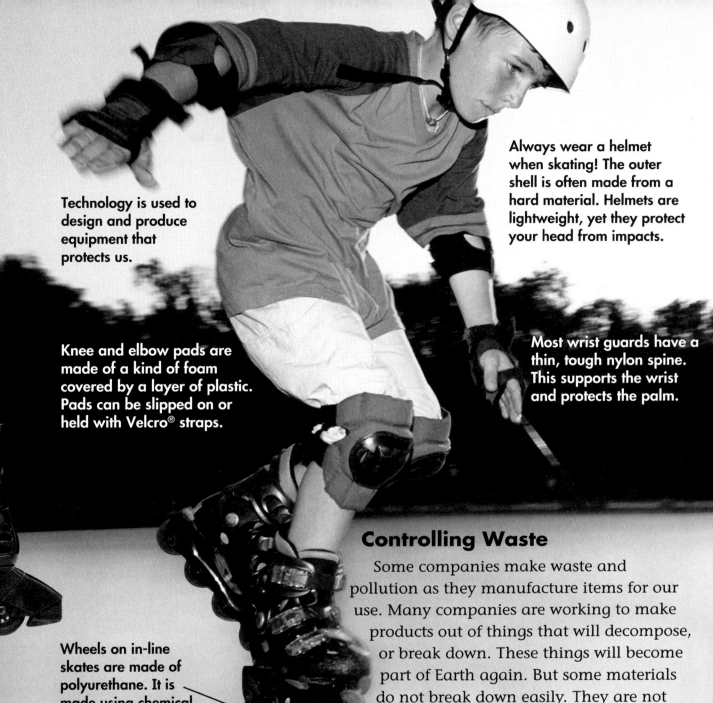

Technology is used to design and produce equipment that protects us.

Always wear a helmet when skating! The outer shell is often made from a hard material. Helmets are lightweight, yet they protect your head from impacts.

Knee and elbow pads are made of a kind of foam covered by a layer of plastic. Pads can be slipped on or held with Velcro® straps.

Most wrist guards have a thin, tough nylon spine. This supports the wrist and protects the palm.

Wheels on in-line skates are made of polyurethane. It is made using chemical technology.

Controlling Waste

Some companies make waste and pollution as they manufacture items for our use. Many companies are working to make products out of things that will decompose, or break down. These things will become part of Earth again. But some materials do not break down easily. They are not part of nature because they have been made by people. In fact, they have been made through technology. We should recycle plastic, glass, aluminum, and other materials that are the results of technology.

1. ✓ Checkpoint How did an item found in nature play a role in the invention of Velcro®?

2. ⟳ Main Idea and Details Which details support the main idea that in-line skating gear is made from many different materials?

553

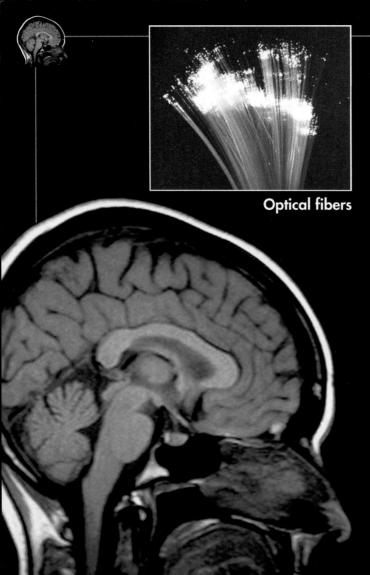

Optical fibers

Technology and Medicine

Medical technology has greatly changed the tools that are used to treat illness and injuries. The changes have improved medical care. Now, instead of using small, sharp knives in operations, doctors sometimes use lasers. A laser beam can remove tissue. It can unclog blocked arteries and fix broken blood vessels.

Today, doctors often use tools with **optical fibers.** These very thin tubes allow light to pass through them. Doctors use cameras with optical fibers to see inside the body without making a large cut. They can decide what the problem is and the best way to treat it. Sometimes they decide that very little surgery is needed inside the body.

Keyhole surgery is one way that technology has improved the care doctors are able to give. The patient may have less pain and heal faster because the doctor makes only a small cut, about the size of a keyhole.

Technology and Food

You know that proper nutrition is part of good health. Nature provides food. Technology gives us some control over nature. People in many areas use tractors, chemical fertilizers, and pesticides. They are able to grow many kinds of plants. The crops they harvest provide different foods needed for a healthy diet.

But with these good things come drawbacks, too. The same fertilizers and pesticides that help crops grow can harm the environment.

The harvester allows the grain from huge fields to be gathered—quickly!

X rays and More

Machines that help doctors determine what is wrong are a great step forward in medicine. Perhaps you know someone who has had an X ray of a broken bone. After the doctor sees where the bone is broken and what the break looks like, fixing the bone is easier.

People make machines to do things they would not be able to do in other ways. In 1895, Wilhelm Roentgen (1845–1923) discovered X rays. He did not understand his discovery right away. In science, X is a symbol for the unknown. Roentgen called his finding X rays. For the first time, doctors saw inside the body—without touching it!

Have you had your teeth X-rayed at your dentist's office? An X-ray picture shows the dentist where a cavity may be forming. Doctors take X rays to find broken bones or tumors. X rays are also used to treat cancer. But the same technology that is so helpful can be harmful, too. Too much contact with X rays can cause burns and cancer.

Today, Nuclear Magnetic Resonance, or NMR technology, allows doctors to identify the chemical makeup of matter. They can use magnetic resonance imaging (MRI) technology to learn about things that don't show up on X rays. They can get a detailed look at what is happening inside blood vessels, for example.

How X Rays Work
X rays pass through skin and other organs. Bones, metal, and other objects block the rays and cast clear shadows on film. We call the shadow picture an X ray.

✓ Lesson Checkpoint

1. How do doctors use new medical technology in surgeries?
2. Compare and contrast the benefits of X rays with the harmful qualities.
3. **Writing** in Science **Descriptive** You are a doctor living in 1895. You have just seen Wilhelm Roentgen demonstrate a new X-ray machine. Write an entry in your **science journal** to describe what you saw. Include your thoughts about this new technology.

How has technology changed communication and transportation?

We depend on communication and transportation. Without technology, communications would be limited. Transportation would not run.

Communication

Have you called someone, written a letter, sent an email or an Instant Message lately? Then you have communicated! **Communication** is the process of sending any type of message from one place to another. You communicate to have your needs met and to stay safe and well. You also communicate to interact with other people. You may use speech or writing. But there are many other ways to get your message across.

Good communication takes three things. You must send a message. The message must be received. And it must be understood. Sending an email through the World Wide Web is one example of the process. But without technology, speech only goes a short way. As time passes, we may not remember all the details of the original spoken message.

Can you think of other ways to send messages? By writing, you can send them with ink and paper. With speech, you can use a phone. With photography, you can use a camera. Without technology, communication is limited. After the invention of writing about 8,000 years ago, messages could be sent long distances, and the ideas in them could be stored for a long time. But the messages had to be written by hand.

A quill—the hollow shaft of a feather—was first used as a pen around A.D. 600.

Dried and cleaned goose, swan, or turkey feathers were most popular. Their thick shafts held the ink. The tip was shaved to a point with a knife.

By 1455, a German goldsmith, Johannes Gutenberg, had invented a way of making type with single letters. Hard metal punches were carved with letters.

In Gutenberg's workshop, workers set movable letter blocks by hand. After they printed as many copies as they needed, the letters could be reused. Printing brought the benefits of writing to a wider group.

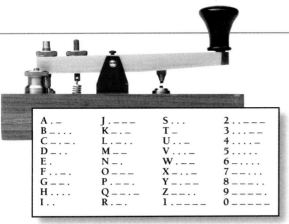

A .-	J .---	S ...	2 ..---
B -...	K -.-	T -	3 ...--
C -.-.	L .-..	U ..-	4 ....-
D -..	M --	V ...-	5 .....
E .	N -.	W .--	6 -....
F ..-.	O ---	X -..-	7 --...
G --.	P .--.	Y -.--	8 ---..
H	Q --.-	Z --..	9 ----.
I ..	R .-.	1 .----	0 -----

The earliest form of telecommunication was the electric telegraph. An electric current shot along a wire in short bursts called Morse code.

Early motion picture cameras used film that moved from one reel to another reel. After the film was developed, another machine was needed to view it.

Telecommunications

Communication paired with electricity completely changed the way of life in the 19th century. The time that passed between a message being sent and received shrank. Messages that used to take several days or even weeks arrived in seconds. In time, people could talk from one continent to another. The world became smaller, the pace of life faster. Today, many forms of communication take only a split second to reach hundreds of people.

Telecommunications are communications that are done electronically. A transmitter sends out a signal with information. The signal travels to a receiver. The receiver turns that signal back into a clear message. Communication satellites send telephone, radio, TV, and other signals from one part of Earth to another. They are also used for navigation by cars, trucks, aircraft, and ships.

Early video cameras took moving pictures and could also play them back.

1. ✓**Checkpoint** In what ways did life change when electricity was used with communication?
2. **Social Studies** in Science Use sources such as nonfiction books, encyclopedias, and the Internet to discover more about methods of communication. Make a poster, a diagram, or a model, to share your findings.

Transportation Systems

Transportation systems move people and goods from place to place. Most transportation systems use a vehicle. A **vehicle** carries the people and goods. Cars, trucks, trains, ships, planes, and rockets are vehicles. Vehicles move on roadways, railways, and waterways, and through airways. Long trips that once took days or weeks may now take only hours. Which vehicles have you traveled in or on?

To make vehicles safe, engineers test and improve new designs. Seat belts, air bags, and new bumpers make safer cars. But, the extra costs of making safety items means that the car costs more to buy.

1807: Robert Fulton builds the *Clermont.* It is the first steamboat that carries passengers—and stays in business.

1890s: Electric trolley streetcars begin to replace horse-drawn trolleys for public transportation in cities.

1914: Henry Ford's factory mass produces automobiles. More people can afford to own a car.

1869: The transcontinental railroad across the United States links the east and the west. The railroad is completed at Promontory, Utah. The last spike is made of gold.

1903: Bicycle makers Orville and Wilbur Wright build a powered airplane. Orville flies 120 feet in 12 seconds.

Have you seen a conveyor belt? Have you ever taken an escalator or elevator? These systems are also designed, built, run, and used by people.

Today's transportation systems often use computer technology. Computers keep systems running properly and on time. Space transportation systems use computer technology, too. Scientists use computers and computer models to solve problems of great distances, weightlessness, and airlessness.

The Technology of Time Measurement

Time can be measured in the seconds it takes to move parts from one place to another on an assembly line. It can be the days a truck takes to cross the continent or the weeks a huge cargo ship takes to cross the ocean. Keeping track of time has always been important to us. In ancient Egypt, astronomers used the Sun's movement to tell time. Later, people used machines that repeated mechanical motions again and again. Today, we use clocks and watches that can measure time in fractions of seconds.

1959: Transcontinental jet service connects New York City and Los Angeles.

Early 1980s: Articulated buses carry passengers in cities in North America.

1937: British inventor Sir Frank Whittle builds the first successful jet engine.

1964: High-speed electric "bullet trains" begin operating in Japan.

2004: In Shanghai, China, the world's first commercial maglev rail system begins operating.

✓ Lesson Checkpoint

1. How does the way we measure time today differ from the way the ancient Egyptians measured it?

2. 🎯 **Main Idea and Details** What are some details that support the main idea that most modern transportation systems use vehicles?

Investigate Why are satellite antennas curved?

Materials

index card

scissors

metric ruler

foil

round bowl

black paper

clay and flashlight

Process Skills

You can use what you **observe** and what you already know to make an **inference.**

What to Do

1 Cut out 4 slits in an index card.

Use clay to hold the index card straight up.

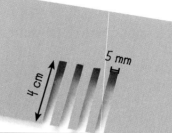

4 cm

5 mm

Use clay to tip the flashlight slightly downward.

about 45 cm

2 Fold the square of foil twice in half to make a strip as shown.

Do not wrinkle the foil!

3 Bend the foil around the bowl to make a smooth curve.

bend

4 In a dark room turn on the flashlight. **Observe** how the light reflects off the foil. Find where the light comes together at one spot. If necessary, slightly curve the foil closer together or farther apart.

5 Copy and complete the drawing. Use dotted lines to show how the light reflects off the foil.

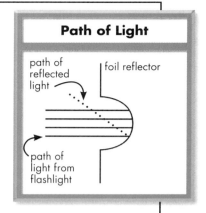

Path of Light

path of reflected light

foil reflector

path of light from flashlight

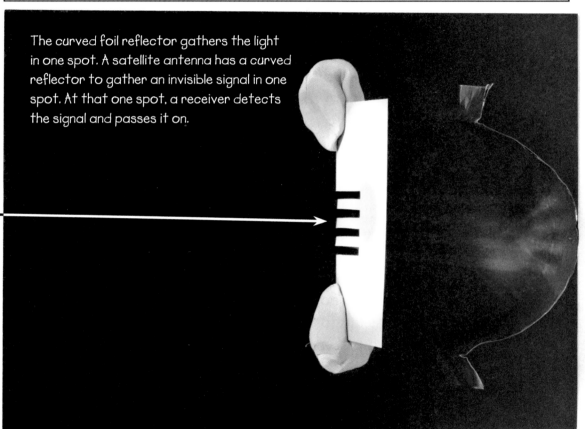

The curved foil reflector gathers the light in one spot. A satellite antenna has a curved reflector to gather an invisible signal in one spot. At that one spot, a receiver detects the signal and passes it on.

Explain Your Results

1. **Infer** If a very weak signal were coming from space, would you need a large or small satellite antenna to detect it?

2. Compare and contrast your model of a satellite antenna with the real thing.

3. Explain why a satellite antenna is curved.

Go Further

What would be the effect of a more powerful signal or a larger antenna? Change your model to help answer this or other questions you may have.

Scale Models and Scale Drawings

Inventors, architects, and designers often make a scale model or a scale drawing. This helps them when they design new products. A scale model or scale drawing is exactly like the new product it represents, but either much larger or much smaller. A scale is a special type of ratio. A ratio compares two quantities. If there are 12 boys and 15 girls in your class, the ratio of boys to girls would be 12 to 15. Ratios can be written several ways: 12 to 15, 12:15, or $\frac{12}{15}$. A scale compares size on a model to size on the actual object.

This model of a solar powered car has a scale of 1 cm : 25 cm. That means that a length of 1 cm on the model represents a length of 25 cm on the actual car. If the model is 10 cm long, how long is the actual car?

$$\frac{1 \text{ cm}}{25 \text{ cm}} = \frac{10 \text{ cm}}{?}$$ Write the ratios in fraction form.

$$\frac{1 \times 10}{25 \times 10} = \frac{10}{250}$$ Work with equivalent ratios in the same way as equivalent fractions.

The actual car is 250 cm long.

A map is a scale drawing. Any distance on the map is much less than the actual distance it represents.

A map has a scale of 1 cm : 4 km. Two cities are shown 5 cm apart on the map. What is the actual distance between the two cities?

$$\frac{1 \text{ cm}}{4 \text{ km}} = \frac{5 \text{ cm}}{?}$$

$$\frac{1 \text{ cm} \times 5}{4 \text{ km} \times 5} = \frac{5 \text{ cm}}{20 \text{ km}}$$

The actual distance between the cities is 20 kilometers.

Use the model car on page 562 and the map described above to answer each question.

1. If the model car is 5 cm wide, how wide is the actual car?

2. If the model car is 3 cm tall, how tall is the actual car?

3. Two rivers are 6 cm apart on the map. What is the actual distance between the rivers?

4. The mapmaker wanted to draw a line showing a straight road that is actually 36 km long. How long should the line be on the map?

Lab zone Take-Home Activity

Make a scale model or scale drawing of a room in your house. You will need to find the actual measurements of the room and everything in it. Decide on a scale to use. Then find the measurements for the model or drawing.

Chapter 19 Review and Test Prep

Use Vocabulary

communication (p. 556)	technology (p. 551)
optical fibers (p. 554)	telecommuni-cations (p. 557)
	vehicle (p. 558)

Use the term from the list above that best completes each sentence.

1. _____ are messages that are sent by electronic means.

2. A(n) _____ carries people and objects from one place to another.

3. Very thin tubes that let light pass through them are _____.

4. _____ is the knowledge, processes, and products that we use to make our lives better.

5. Writing a letter to a pen pal is an example of _____.

Explain Concepts

6. Explain how a machine or tool has helped people do something they could not do without it.

7. Explain how one scientific advance might have been influenced by or related to an earlier one.

8. Explain how technology in medicine has helped both doctors and patients.

Process Skills

9. **Infer** Employees of a small company take orders over the phone. They enter the orders in a computer program that sends them to be filled. The company buys a new computer system. Now customers enter their own orders. Why might the company and its employees have very different reactions to the new system?

10. **Make a model** that shows how creating technology to solve one problem might cause other unexpected problems.

11. **Predict** how transportation technology might develop even more advanced ways of moving people and objects. Explain how you arrived at your ideas.

12. **Form a hypothesis** Velcro® was invented after a scientist pulled burs off his clothes and his dog. How do you think Post-it® notes may have been invented?

MindPoint Quiz Show

Main Idea and Details

13. Make a graphic organizer like the one shown below. Fill in the missing details that support the main idea.

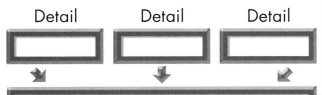

Detail	Detail	Detail

The way people communicate has changed a great deal over time.

Test Prep

Choose the letter that best completes the statement or answers the question.

14. Through technology, we have materials that do not appear in
  Ⓐ science.
  Ⓑ medicine.
  Ⓒ nature.
  Ⓓ telecommunications.

15. In the 1800s, the way of life changed when _____ was used with communication.
  Ⓕ electricity
  Ⓖ television
  Ⓗ time
  Ⓘ transportation

16. Throughout history, people have used various ways to keep track of
  Ⓐ optical fibers.
  Ⓑ telecommunications.
  Ⓒ lasers.
  Ⓓ time.

17. Sometimes technology can cause
  Ⓕ distances to seem greater.
  Ⓖ unexpected problems.
  Ⓗ us to stop making machines.
  Ⓘ the pace of life to slow down.

18. Which has brought people closer together?
  Ⓐ optical fibers
  Ⓑ clocks and watches
  Ⓒ standard time zones
  Ⓓ modern transportation

19. Explain why the answer you selected for Question 17 is best. For each answer you did not select, give a reason why it is not the best choice.

20. **Writing in Science** **Persuasive** What is the best or worst effect of technology? Use words that will persuade others to share your opinion.

Telemedicine

When you are sick, your mother or father might take you to the doctor. The doctor has learned how to help make you feel better and has the special tools he or she needs to find out what is wrong. What if you lived in a place that was far from a doctor? Your parent could call a doctor who would tell her or him what to do. The problem is that your parent doesn't have the same special tools a doctor has to examine you.

This same problem applies to astronauts in space. They are many miles from the nearest doctor. NASA is developing technologies to solve this problem. Computers, satellites, and digital imaging technology help astronauts talk, write, and send pictures to doctors on Earth. The information the doctors receive helps them decide how to care for the astronauts in space.

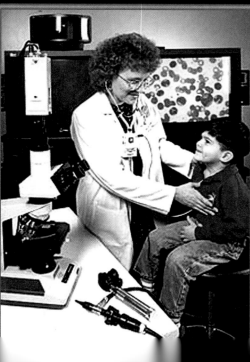

Astronaut Guion Bluford monitors his blood pressure. This information is recorded to track his health while in space.

In the same way that astronauts in space can "visit" doctors on Earth, people in areas far from cities can "visit" a doctor. Some places on Earth have very few doctors. Other places do not have doctors who have special training to treat specific illnesses. NASA is working with businesses, hospitals, and doctors to solve this problem. They are using a process called telemedicine. It means giving medical help to people who are far away.

One place that uses telemedicine is Harlingen, Texas. Some people in Harlingen need help from doctors in San Antonio. Traveling 250 miles to San Antonio is expensive, difficult, and takes a lot of time. NASA and several businesses have worked together to provide telemedicine facilities for this area. Doctors from South Texas Hospital in Harlingen can send patient information such as heart rate, blood pressure, or X-ray images to doctors in San Antonio. After the medical specialists in San Antonio study the information, they can tell the doctors in Harlingen how to make their patients better.

The technology that NASA is developing is helping people all over the world receive better medical care.

Lab zone Take-Home Activity

With your family, look for objects that have *tele-* as part of their name. What do these objects have in common?

Otis Boykin

Inventor Otis Boykin

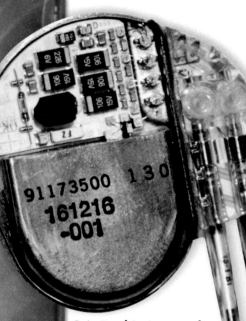

Otis Boykin invented part of the pacemaker. Placed near the heart, the pacemaker helps the heart beat in rhythm.

The pacemaker is a great tool in medical technology. It is an electronic device that runs on batteries. Strange though it may sound, it sends electric shocks to the heart! It keeps the heart beating at the proper rhythm. The hearts of people who have heart disease do not work properly. The heart slows down or beats too fast. For them, the pacemaker is a lifesaver. It keeps their hearts beating just right. And they have Otis Boykin to thank.

Otis Boykin (1920–1982) grew up in Dallas, Texas. After graduating from Fisk University in Nashville, Tennessee, Boykin worked in Chicago, Illinois. It was not long, though, before he began inventing! He invented the electrical devices used in all guided missiles and in computers. All together, Boykin made 26 electrical devices. One was part of the pacemaker.

Have you heard the word *ironic* before? Something that is ironic is the opposite of what you would expect. Sadly, it is quite ironic that Otis Boykin, the inventor of a major part of the pacemaker, died of a heart attack.

Lab zone Take-Home Activity

Design a device that could help people in some way. Use ordinary materials to make

Unit D Test Talk

Write Your Answer

To answer the following test questions, you need to write your answer. Read the passage and then answer the questions.

For centuries people have watched the stars move across the sky. Ancient sky-watchers noticed patterns in how certain groups of stars moved. Perhaps they thought the star groups formed pictures. Modern astronomers have divided the sky into 88 constellations. A constellation is a group of stars in a certain region of the sky. Many of the constellations are named by a pattern of stars in that region. Many stars are identified by the constellation they are part of. The stars in each constellation may look close together, but they are really far apart.

Stars can tell you the time whether you are on land, on sea, or in the air. You can watch constellations rise and set at the time and place you expect. The paths of the constellations moving across the sky are the same year after year.

Astronomers classify stars according to size, brightness, or temperature. To us, the Sun is the most important star in the sky. Many stars are cooler, smaller, and dimmer than the Sun. But some stars are hotter, bigger, or brighter.

Stars appear to be different colors because of the temperature of their atmosphere. The hottest stars are blue. The temperature of blue stars is at least 11,000°C. The star Rigel in the Orion constellation is blue. The next hottest stars are white, followed by yellowish-white and then yellow. The Sun is a yellow star. Its temperature ranges from 5100°C to 6,000°C. The temperature of orange stars is between 3600°C and 5100°C. Red stars, such as Betelgeuse in Orion, are the coolest of all. Their temperature is between 2000°C and 3600°C.

Use What You Know

To write your answer to each question, you need to read the passage and the test question carefully. Write complete sentences. Then read your answer to make sure it is complete, correct, and focused.

1. How does the Sun compare with other stars?
2. Sirius is a white star. It is the brightest star in the sky. How do you know it is not the hottest?
3. What is a constellation?
4. Suppose last night you helped your friend locate Orion in the sky. How will your friend know where to find Orion a year from now?

Unit D Wrap-Up

Chapter 17

How are cycles on Earth affected by the Sun and the Moon?

- Earth's movement around the Sun and Earth's tilt cause the seasons.
- The shape of the Moon appears to change as it revolves around Earth.
- Eclipses occur as a result of the Moon revolving around Earth.
- Earth's rotation is the reason groups of stars seem to move across the sky.

Chapter 18

How is Earth different from the other parts of the solar system?

- The part of the universe known as the solar system is made up of the Sun, planets, moons, other objects, and mostly empty space.
- Each planet in the solar system rotates on its axis and revolves around the Sun.
- Some planets have similar characteristics.

Chapter 19

How do the devices and products of technology affect the way we live?

- Advances in technology make our work easier and give us products that keep us safe and comfortable.
- Faster systems of transportation and communication are results of technology.

Performance Assessment

How Technology Helps Scientists

Give examples of technology that helps scientists learn about Earth and space. Make drawings or models that show the technology and write a brief description of what scientists have learned by using the technology.

Read More About Space and Technology

Look for books such as these in the library.

Lab zone **Full Inquiry**

Experiment How does payload affect the distance a model rocket can travel?

Rockets launched from Earth have carried satellites, telescopes, and astronauts into space. The mass a rocket can carry is called its payload. In this experiment you will make a model rocket and find out how the payload affects the distance a model rocket travels.

Materials

safety goggles

Rocket Pattern and scissors

tape and 2 L plastic bottle

straw and clay

4 large paper clips

meterstick

Process Skills

You **control variables** when you change only one thing in an **experiment.**

Ask a question.

How does the payload affect the distance a model rocket can travel?

State a hypothesis.

If you increase the payload, then will the distance a model rocket travels remain the same, increase, or decrease? Write your **hypothesis**.

Identify and control variables.

You will change the payload your model rocket carries by changing the number of paper clips taped to the rocket. You will measure the distance the rocket travels. Everything else must remain the same. Always (a) use the same rocket, (b) launch the rocket from the same place, at the same height, and at the same angle, and (c) squeeze the bottle with the same force.

Think about the **variables** in your **experiment.**
    What is the independent variable?
    What is the dependent variable?
    What are some controlled variables?

Test your hypothesis.

Make a model of a rocket.

1 Cut out the Rocket Pattern.

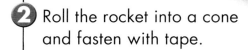

2 Roll the rocket into a cone and fasten with tape.

3 Make a launcher. Place a straw about 4 cm into a 2 L bottle. Seal the opening around the straw with clay.

Be careful!

Wear safety goggles! Why do you think you must wear safety goggles?

4 cm

4 Put the rocket on the launcher.

⑤ Squish!

Launch your rocket 3 times. **Measure** the distances the rocket travels. Record the farthest distance.

Hold your rocket launcher in the same position for each launch. Squeeze the bottle with the same force each time.

Be careful!

Make sure no one is in the way when you launch your rocket!

⑥ Repeat your test with 2 large paper clips taped to your rocket. Tape the paper clips on the side of the rocket, at the top.

⑦ Repeat your test with 4 large paper clips taped to your rocket.

Hold the bottle at this angle every time.

Collect and record your data.

Payload (number of paper clips)	Farthest Distance Rocket Traveled (cm)
0	
2	
4	

Interpret your data.

Use your data to make a bar graph. Look at your graph closely. Analyze how the number of paper clips carried by your rocket affected the distance it traveled.

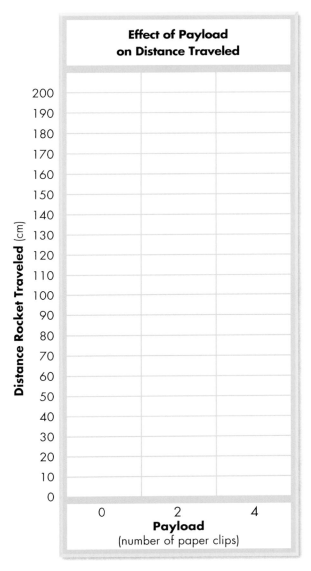

Effect of Payload on Distance Traveled

Distance Rocket Traveled (cm): 200, 190, 180, 170, 160, 150, 140, 130, 120, 110, 100, 90, 80, 70, 60, 50, 40, 30, 20, 10, 0

Payload (number of paper clips): 0, 2, 4

What pattern do you find in your data? What is a reasonable explanation for the results of your experiment?

State your conclusion.

Explain how the payload affected the distance your model rocket traveled. Compare your hypothesis with your results. **Communicate** your conclusion.

Go Further

How would adding fins affect how far the rocket travels? Write and carry out a plan to investigate. Develop a hypothesis. Include a safety procedure. Keep a record in a science journal. Select a way to show your results. Write a report or share your results orally with your class.

Full Inquiry

Using Scientific Methods
1. Ask a question.
2. State a hypothesis.
3. Identify and control variables.
4. Test your hypothesis.
5. Collect and record your data.
6. Interpret your data.
7. State your conclusion.
8. Go further.

How Heavy Is Heavy?
Idea: Weigh an object such as a heavy shoe to determine its Earth weight. Figure out how much the object would weigh on each of the other planets in the solar system. Use the information to make an exhibit that shows the weight of the object on Earth and its weight on each of the other planets.

Objects in Space
Idea: Make models of the planets and other space objects. Be sure to tell if your model shows the relative sizes or the relative distances of the objects. Make a poster that includes at least one interesting fact about each object.

Phases of the Moon
Idea: Make a flipbook to show how the phases of the Moon change during the month. Make drawings that show how the Moon looks each day of the month. Then put them in order to make the booklet. Check to be sure the pages are firmly attached before you flip them.

What Time Is It?
Idea: Find the latitude of your home. Use the latitude to make a sundial. Show how shadows cast by the sundial can be used to tell time.

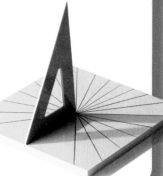

EC NTL 10 9 8 7 6 5 4 3

Metric and Customary Measurement

The metric system is the measurement system most commonly used in science. Metric units are sometimes called SI units. SI stands for International System. It is called that because these units are used around the world.

These prefixes are used in the metric system:

kilo- means *thousand*
1 kilometer equals 1,000 meters

milli- means *one thousandth*
1,000 millimeters equals 1 meter or 1 millimeter = 0.001 meter

centi- means *one hundredth*
100 centimeters equals 1 meter or 1 centimeter = 0.01 meter

Length and Distance

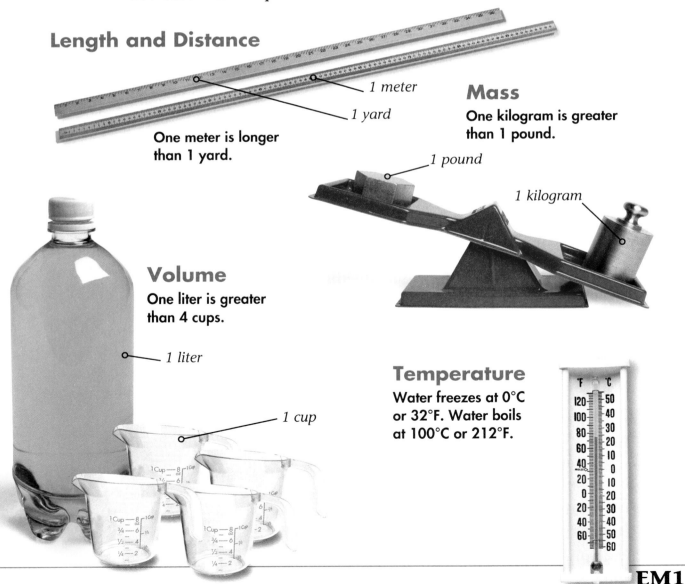

1 meter

1 yard

One meter is longer than 1 yard.

Mass

One kilogram is greater than 1 pound.

1 pound

1 kilogram

Volume

One liter is greater than 4 cups.

1 liter

1 cup

Temperature

Water freezes at 0°C or 32°F. Water boils at 100°C or 212°F.

Glossary

The glossary uses letters and signs to show how words are pronounced. The mark ′ is placed after a syllable with a primary or heavy accent. The mark ′ is placed after a syllable with a secondary or lighter acdcent.

To hear these words pronounced, listen to the AudioText CD.

absorption (ab sôrp′shən) the taking in of light energy by an object (p. 420)

adaptation (ad′ap tā′shən) trait that helps a living thing survive in its environment (p. 26)

anemometer (an′ə mom′ə tər) a tool that measures wind speed (p. 195)

astronomy (ə stron′ə mē) the study of planets, stars, and other objects in space (p. 519)

atmosphere (at′mə sfir) the blanket of gases that surrounds Earth (p. 188)

atom (at′əm) one of the tiny particles that make up all of matter (p. 375)

axis (ak′sis) an imaginary line that goes through an object; Earth's axis goes through the North and South Poles (p. 496)

barometer (bə rom′ə tər) a tool that measures air pressure (p. 194)

C

carnivores (kär′nə vôrz) consumers that eat only animals (p. 84)

cause (kȯz) why something happens (p. 109)

cell (sel) the building block of life (p. 7)

change of state (chānj ov stāt) physical change in matter caused by a different arrangement or movement of particles (p. 320)

chemical change (kem′ə kəl chānj) a change that results in a new substance (p. 336)

chlorophyll (klôr′ə fil) green material in plants that captures energy from sunlight for photosynthesis (p. 49)

chloroplast (klôr′ə plast) a special part of a plant that traps the energy in sunlight for making food (p. 8)

classifying (klas′ə fī ing) arranging or sorting objects, events, or living things according to their properties (p. 34)

collecting data (kə lekt′ing dā′tə) gathering observations and measurements (p. 108)

communicating (kə myü′nə kāt ing) using words, pictures, charts, graphs, and diagrams to share information (p. 180)

communication (kə myü′nə kā′shən) the process of sending any type of message from one place to another (p. 556)

community (kə myü′nə tē) different populations that interact with each other in the same area (p. 82)

compare (kəm pâr′) to say how things are alike (p. 5)

competition (kom′pə tish′ən) two or more living things in an ecosystem using the same limited resources (p. 114)

EM2

compression (kəm presh′ən) the pushing together of a mass so that it occupies less space (p. 408)

conclusion (kən klü′zhən) a decision reached after thinking about facts and details (p. 45)

condensation (kon′den sā′shən) the process of water vapor, a gas, changing to a liquid (p. 187)

conduction (kən duk′shən) the transfer or passing of energy (p. 354)

conductor (kən duk′tər) a material that allows thermal energy or electricity to pass through it (p. 354)

conservation (kon′sər vā′shən) using only what you need as efficiently as possible (p. 296)

constellation (kon′stə lā′ shən) any one of 88 areas in the sky that are used to identify and name the stars (p. 504)

consumer (kən sü′mər) living things that eat other organisms (p. 84)

contrast (kən trast′) to say how things are different (p. 5)

convection current (kən vek′shən kėr′ənt) the pattern in which thermal energy flows; formed when heated liquid or gas expands and is less dense than a cooler liquid or gas around it (p. 356)

crater (krā′tər) a large hole shaped like a bowl in the surface of Earth, another planet, a moon, or other object in space (p. 270)

cytoplasm (sī′tə plaz′əm) a gel-like liquid inside the cell membrane that contains the things that the cell needs (p. 8)

decomposers (dē′kəm pō′zərz) organisms that live and grow by breaking down the waste and remains of dead plants and animals to obtain nutrients (p. 87)

density (den′sə tē) the property of matter that compares the mass of an object to its volume (p. 326)

deposition (dep′ə zish′ən) the laying down of rock, soil, organic matter, or other material on the surface of Earth (p. 267)

details (di tālz′) individual pieces of information that support a main idea (p. 213)

dormant (dôr′mənt) in a state of rest (p. 62)

earthquake (ėrth′kwāk′) a shaking of Earth's crust or lithosphere caused by sudden, shifting movements in the crust (p. 272)

eclipse (i klips′) a temporary situation in which an object in space casts its shadow on another object (p. 502)

ecosystem (ē′kō sis′təm) all the living and nonliving things in an environment and the many ways they interact (p. 79)

effect (ə feckt′) what happens as a result of a cause (p. 109)

effort (ef′ərt) the force used on a simple machine (p. 464)

electric current (i lek′trik kėr′ənt) the flow of an electric charge through a material (p. 378)

electromagnet (i lek′trō mag′nit) a coil of wire that causes a magnetic field when current moves through the wire (p. 387)

element (el′ə mənt) matter that has only one kind of atom (p. 337)

ellipse (i lips′) an oval-shaped curve that is like a circle stretched out in opposite directions (p. 498)

endangered (en dān′jərd) a species whose population has been reduced to such small numbers that it is in danger of becoming extinct (p. 120)

energy (en′ər jē) the ability to do work or to cause a change (p. 84)

energy transfer (en′ər jē tran′sfėr′) the flow of energy in a food chain from the producer to prey to predator (p. 86)

environment (en vī′rən mənt) everything that surrounds a living thing (p. 118)

epicenter (ep′ə sen′tər) the point on Earth's surface directly above the focus of an earthquake (p. 272)

equator (i kwā′ tər) the imaginary line that separates the northern and southern halves of Earth (p. 499)

erosion (i rō′zhən) the moving of pieces of soil or rock by mechanisms including gravity, wind, water, ice, or plants or animals (p. 266)

estimating and measuring (es′tə māt ing and mezh′ər ing) telling how large you think an object is and then finding out its exact size (p. 308)

evaporation (i vap′ə rā′shən) the change from liquid water to water vapor (p. 186)

experiment (ek sper′ə ment) to formulate and test a hypothesis using a scientific method (p. 172)

explore (ek splôr′) to study a scientific idea in a hands-on manner (p. 4)

extinct (ek stingkt′) no longer living, as an entire species, or no longer active, as a volcano (p. 120)

fault (fôlt) a break or crack in Earth where the rocks on one side have moved relative to the rocks on the other side (p. 272)

fertilization (fèr′tl ə zā′shən) the process by which an egg cell and a sperm cell combine (p. 56)

food chain (füd chān) the process by which energy moves from one type of living thing to another (p. 86)

food web (füd web) a system of overlapping food chains in which the flow of energy branches out in many directions (p. 88)

force (fôrs) any push or pull (p. 442)

forming questions and hypotheses (fôrm′ing kwes′chənz and hī poth′ə səz′) thinking of how you can solve a problem or answer a question (p. 484)

fossil (fos′əl) remains or mark of a living thing from long ago (p. 244)

fossil fuels (fos′əl fyü′əlz) fuels including coal, petroleum, and natural gas that are made from fossils, or the remains of living things that died millions of years ago (p. 294)

frame of reference (frām uv ref′ər əns) objects that don't seem to move define your frame of reference (p. 440)

frequency (frē′kwən sē) the number of times a wave makes a complete cycle in a second (p. 409)

friction (frik′shən) force that acts when two surfaces rub together (p. 445)

front (frunt) the boundary across which two different air masses touch another (p. 190)

fulcrum (ful′krəm) the support on which a lever plus its load rests (p. 464)

galaxy (gal′ək sē) system of millions to trillions of stars held together by the force of gravity (p. 519)

gas (gas) one of the states of matter which takes the shape of its container and expands to whatever space is available (p. 321)

genus (jē′nəs) a grouping that contains similar, closely related animals (p. 12)

gravity (grav′ə tē) an attractive force between two or more objects over a distance. The more mass an object has, the stronger the gravitational force. (p. 519)

habitat (hab′ə tat) area or place where an organism lives in an ecosystem (p. 82)

hazardous waste (haz′ər dəs wāst) substances that are very harmful to humans and other organisms (p. 126)

heat (hēt) the transfer of thermal energy between matter with different temperatures (p. 354)

herbivores (ėr′bə vôrz) consumers that get energy by eating only plants (p. 84)

host (hōst) an organism that is harmed by a parasite (p. 117)

humidity (hyü mid′ə tē) the amount of water vapor in the air (p. 190)

humus (hyü′mas) a dark brown part of soil that is made up of decomposed plants and animals (p. 289)

hurricane (hėr′ə kān) a dangerous storm made up of swirling bands of thunderstorms with wind speeds of at least 119 km per hour (p. 215)

identifying and controlling variables (ī den′tə fī ing and kən trōl′ing vâr′ē ə bəlz) changing one thing, but keep all the other factors the same (p. 172)

igneous rock (ig′nē əs rok′) rock that forms from molten (melted) rock (p. 246)

immune system (i myün′ sis′təm) the organs in your body that defend against disease (p. 161)

inclined plane (in klīnd′ plān) a simple machine like a ramp (p. 12)

infectious disease (in fek′shəs də zēz′) a disease that can pass from one organism to another (p. 158)

inferring (in fėr′ing) drawing a conclusion or making a reasonable guess based on what you have learned or what you know (p. 66)

insulator (in′sə lā′tər) a material or substance that limits the amount of heat that passes through it (p. 355)

interpreting data (in tėr′prit ing dā′tə) using the information you have collected to solve problems or answer questions (p. 200)

invertebrates (in vėr′tə brits) animals without backbones (p. 22)

investigate (in ves′tə gāt) to solve a problem or answer a question by following an existing procedure or an original one (p. 96)

investigating and experimenting (in ves′tə gāt ing and ek sper′ə ment ing) planning and doing an investigation to test a hypothesis or solve a problem (p. 484)

involuntary muscles (in vol′ən ter′ē mus′əlz) muscles that you cannot control (p. 146)

kinetic energy (kin net′ik en′ər jē) energy of motion (p. 448)

landform (land′fôrm′) a natural feature on Earth's surface; landforms include mountains, hills, valleys, plains, plateaus, and coastal features (p. 263)

landslide (land′slīd) a rapid downhill movement of large amounts of rock and soil (p. 268)

lever (lev′ər) a simple machine made of a bar resting on a fulcrum (p. 464)

life cycle (līf sī′kəl) the various stages through which an organism passes from birth as it grows, matures, and dies (p. 20)

light (līt) a form of energy that travels in waves and can affect properties of matter (p. 418)

liquid (lik′wid) one of the states of matter which does not have a definite shape but takes up a definite amount of space (p. 321)

load (lōd) the weight that is to be lifted or moved (p. 464)

lunar eclipse (lü′nər i klips′) the passage of the Moon through Earth's shadow (p. 502)

luster (lus′tər) the way a mineral's surface reflects light (p. 240)

magnetic field (mag net′ik fēld) the invisible force that loops between the poles of a magnet due to the arrangement of charges. The force is strongest at the poles, or ends, and gets weaker as distance from the magnet increases. (p. 382)

magnetism (mag′nə tiz′əm) the property of attraction of an object that has a magnetic field. It can attract other objects made of metal (p. 382)

main ideas (mān ī dē′əz) the most important information in a reading passage (p. 213)

making and using models (māk′ing and yüz′ing mod′lz) making a model from materials or making a sketch or a diagram (p. 162)

making operational definitions (māk′ing op′ər ā′shə nəl def′ə nish′ənz) defining or describing an object or event based on your own experience with it (p. 394)

mass (mas) amount of matter in an object (p. 322)

matter (mat′ər) anything that takes up space and has mass (p. 320)

metamorphic rock (met′ə môr′fik rok′) rock that has changed as a result of heating and pressure (p. 248)

meteorologist (mē′tē ə rol′ə jist) a scientist who studies and measures weather conditions (p. 194)

mineral (min′ər əl) natural, nonliving solid crystal that makes up rocks (p. 239)

mixture (miks′chər) a combination of two or more substances that keep their individual properties (p. 328)

moon (mün) a satellite of a planet (p. 524)

Moon phase (mün fāz) the different shapes of the Moon between the time a full Moon is visible and the time when no part of the Moon is visible (p. 501)

neuron (nür′ron) basic working unit of the nervous system or the nerve cell (p. 154)

niche (nich) the specific role an organism has in its habitat (p. 82)

nonrenewable resources (non′ri nü′ə bəl ri sôrs′əz) resource supplies that exist in limited amounts or are used much faster than they can be replaced in nature (p. 294)

nucleus (nü′klē əs) the control center of a cell (p. 8)

observing (əb zėrv′ing) using your senses to find out about objects, events, or living things (p. 4)

omnivores (om′nə vôrz′) consumers that eat both plants and animals (p. 84)

opaque (ō pāk′) describes materials that do not let any light pass through them (p. 421)

optical fibers (op′tə kəl fī′bərz) very thin tubes that allow light to pass through them; often used by doctors in medical procedures (p. 554)

orbit (ôr′bit) the path followed by one object as it revolves around another object, such as Earth's orbit around the Sun (p. 498)

ore (ôr) a mineral-rich rock deposit that can be removed from Earth's crust and used to make products (p. 294)

organ (ôr′gən) a group of tissues working together to carry out body processes (p. 143)

organism (ôr′gə niz′əm) the highest level of cell organization (p. 8)

ovary (ō′vər ē) the thick bottom part of the pistil where the egg cells are stored (p. 56)

parallel circuits (par′ə lel sėr′kits) two or more paths in which an electric charge can flow (p. 381)

parasite (par′ə sīt) an organism that lives on or in another organism, helping itself but hurting the other organism (p. 117)

pathogens (path′ə jənz) organisms that cause disease (p. 158)

petroleum (pə trō′lē əm) a crude oil that is found in rocks; a nonrenewable energy source (p. 294)

photosynthesis (fō′tō sin′thə sis) the process in which plants make their own food (p. 48)

physical change (fiz′ə kəl chānj) a change in the size, shape, or state of matter (p. 332)

pistil (pis′tl) a female structure in plants that produces egg cells (p. 55)

pitch (pich) a measure of whether a sound seems high or low, determined by the sound's frequency (p. 412)

planet (plan′it) a large body of matter that revolves, or travels, around the Sun (p. 540)

pollution (pə lü′shən) waste from products made or used by people (p. 124)

population (pop′yə lā′shən) all the members of one species that live within an area of an ecosystem (p. 82)

potential energy (pə ten′shəl en′ər jē) the amount of energy available to do work because of the way a system is arranged (p. 448)

precipitation (pri sip′ə tā′shən) any form of water falling from the air to Earth's surface (p. 187)

predator (pred′ə tər) a consumer that hunts other animals for food (p. 28)

predict (pri dikt′) make a statement about what might happen next (p. 517)

predicting (pri dikt′ing) telling what you think will happen (p. 66)

prey (prā) any animal hunted by others for food (p. 86)

producer (prə dü′sər) living thing that makes its own food (p. 84)

protist (prō′tist) one-cell organism with a nucleus and other cell parts (p. 11)

pulley (pùl′ē) a simple machine made of a wheel with a rope around it (p. 467)

radiation (rā′dē ā′shən) the transmission of energy as light (p. 358)

recycling (rē sī′kling) saving, collecting, or using materials again instead of turning them into waste (p. 297)

reflection (ri flek′shən) the bouncing back of a wave off an object or surface (p. 420)

refraction (ri frak′shən) bending of a wave caused by the change of speed that occurs when the wave passes from one medium into another (p. 422)

relative motion (rel′ə tiv mō′shən) change in position of one object compared to the position of some fixed object (p. 439)

renewable resource (ri nü′ə bəl ri sôrs′) resource that is endless like sunlight, or that is naturally replaced in a fairly short time, such as trees (p. 287)

resource (ri sôrs′) an important material that living things need (p. 247)

resistance (ri zis′təns) a quality of an object which means that electric current cannot flow easily through it (p. 379)

revolution (rev′ə lü′shən) the repeated motion of one object around another, much more massive object; for instance, the motion of Earth around the Sun (p. 498)

rotation (rō tā′shən) the spinning of a planet, moon, or star around its axis (p. 496)

satellite (sat′l it) something that orbits a planet (p. 524)

scientific method (sī′ən tif′ik meth′əd) organized steps in solving problems (p. xxvi)

screw (skrü) a simple machine made of a stick with ridges wrapped around it (p. 471)

sediment (sed′ə mənt) any earth material that has been moved from one place to another and laid down on the surface of Earth. It includes material moved by gravity, wind, water, ice, or animals and plants (p. 242)

sedimentary rock (sed′ə men′tər ē rok′) rock that forms when sediments are cemented together and harden (p. 242)

sepal (sē′pəl) one of several leaf-like parts that cover and protect the flower bud (p. 55)

sequence (sē′kwəns) the order in which things happen (p. 77)

series circuit (sir′ēz sér′kit) a simple circular path in which an electric current flows only one way through each part of that circuit (p. 380)

solar cells (sō′lər selz) electric cells that convert the Sun's energy into electricity (p. 293)

solar eclipse (sō′lər i klips′) the passage of the Moon between the Sun and Earth; the Moon casts its shadow on Earth (p. 503)

solar energy (sō′lər en′ər jē) the energy transformed from sunlight (p. 287)

solar system (sō′lər sis′təm) a system of planets and other objects that move around the Sun (p. 520)

solid (sol′id) matter that has a definite shape and usually takes up a definite amount of space (p. 321)

solubility (sol′yə bil′ə tē) ability of one substance to dissolve in another (p. 331)

solute (sol′yüt) the substance that is dissolved in a solution (p. 330)

solution (sə lü′shən) a combination of two or more substances where one is dissolved by the other (p. 330)

solvent (sol′vənt) the substance that dissolves another substance in a solution (p. 330)

space probe (spās prōb) a vehicle that carries cameras and other tools for studying distant objects in space (p. 522)

species (spē′shēz) a group of similar organisms that can mate and produce offspring that can reproduce (p. 12)

speed (spēd) the rate at which an object's position changes (p. 440)

stamen (stā′mən) male structure in plants that makes pollen (p. 55)

star (stär) a giant ball of hot, glowing gases (p. 495)

static electricity (stat′ik i lek′tris′ə tē) the imbalance of positive or negative charges between objects (p. 375)

storm surge (stôrm sérj) water pushed ahead onto shore by the winds outside the eye wall of a hurricane (p. 219)

succession (sək sesh′ən) gradual change from one community of organisms to another (p. 118)

summarize (sum′ə riz′) give only the main points (p. 337)

summary (sum′ə rē) a short retelling of something read (p. 237)

Sun (sun) the star that is the central and largest body in the our solar system (p. 521)

system (sis′təm) a set of parts that interact with one another (p. 79)

technology (tek nol′ə jē) the knowledge, processes, and products that we use to solve problems and make our lives easier (p. 551)

telecommunications (tel′ə kə myü′nə kā′shənz) communications sent by telephone, television, satellite, and radio (p. 557)

thermal energy (thér′məl en′ər jē) total energy of motion of particles in a system (p. 351)

tissue (tish′ü) a group of one type of cell (p. 8)

tornado (tôr nā′dō) a rapidly spinning column of air that comes down out of a cloud and touches the ground (p. 222)

translucent (tranz lü′snt) describes materials that let some light rays pass through but scatter some of the other rays (p. 421)

transparent (tran spâr′ənt) describes materials that let nearly all the light rays that hit them pass through (p. 421)

tropical depression (trop′ə kəl di presh′ən) a low pressure air mass that forms over warm water and has swirling winds can be as strong as 61 km per hour (p. 216)

tropical storm (trop′ə kəl stôrm) a low pressure air mass that forms over warm water and has swirling winds that are more than 61 kph but less than 119 kph (p. 216)

universe (yü′nə vérs′) all of the objects that exist in space (p. 519)

vaccine (vak sēn′) an injection of dead or weakened pathogens that causes you to be immune to a disease (p. 161)

vehicle (vē′ə kəl) something that carries people and objects from one place to another such as automobiles, trucks, trains, ships, airplanes, and rockets (p. 558)

velocity (və los′ə tē) the speed and the direction an object is moving (p. 441)

vertebrates (vér′tə brits) animals with backbones (p. 18)

volcano (vol kā′nō) a cone-shaped landform that sometimes releases hot rocks, gases, and ashes (p. 270)

volume (vol′yəm) amount of space matter takes up (p. 324)

voluntary muscles (vol′ən ter′ē mus′əlz) muscles that you can control (p. 146)

vortex (vôr′teks) a spinning, funnel-shaped area in a fluid (p. 223)

water cycle (wȯ′tər sī′kəl) the movement of water from Earth's surface into the air and back again; includes evaporation, condensation and precipitation (p. 186)

wavelength (wāv′lengkth) distance between one point on a wave to the next similar point on a wave (p. 409)

weathering (weŦH′ər ing) a gradual wearing away or changing of rock and soil caused by water, ice, temperature changes, wind, chemicals, or living things (p. 264)

wedge (wej) a simple machine that is made of two inclined planes put together and that can be driven into another material (p. 470)

wheel and axle (wēl and ak′səl) a simple machine made of a wheel and a rod joined to the center of the wheel (p. 466)

wind vane (wind vān) a tool that shows the direction from which the wind is blowing (p. 195)

work (wérk) using force in order to move an object a certain distance (p. 448)

Index

This index lists the pages on which topics appear in this book. Page numbers after a *p* refer to a photograph or drawing. Page numbers after a *c* refer to a chart, graph, or diagram.

Absorption, 402, 420, *p*420

Acid rain, 295

Acids (stomach), 156, *p*156

Active volcano, 271

Activities

Directed Inquiry, Explore, 4, 44, 76, 108, 140, 180, 212, 236, 260, 284, 316, 348, 372, 404, 436, 460, 492, 516, 548

Guided Inquiry Investigate, 34–35, 66–67, 96–97, 130–131, 162–163, 200–201, 226–227, 250–251, 274–275, 298–299, 338–339, 360–361, 394–395, 426–427, 450–451, 474–475, 506–507, 538–539, 560–561

Full Inquiry, Experiment, 172–175, 308–311, 484–487, 572–575

Take-Home Activity 37, 40, 69, 72, 99, 103, 104, 133, 136, 165, 168, 203, 207, 208, 229, 232, 253, 256, 277, 280, 301, 304, 341, 344, 363, 367, 368, 397, 400, 429, 432, 453, 456, 477, 480, 509, 512, 541, 544, 563, 567, 568

Adams, John Couch, 535

Adaptation

animal, 26–27, 28–29

bird, 26

niche of organism and, 82

plant, 60

and role in ecosystem, 84

Air

gases in, 188

measuring with thermometer, *c*352

need for, 111

in respiratory system, 148, *p*149

as solution, 330

Air masses, 190, *c*190

cold front, 191

warm front, 192, *c*192

Airplane, *c*558

Air plants, *c*52

Air pollution, 124, 295

Air pressure, 188, *p*189, *c*194–195, 194–195

Air sac, 148, *c*149

Algae, *p*90

in food web, *c*92

and fungi, 116

Alto **in cloud names,** 193

Altostratus clouds, *c*193

Aluminum recycling, 297, *c*297

Amber, *p*376

American Solar Challenge (ASC) (Department of Energy), 304

Amethyst, 237

Amphibians, 18, *c*18, 29

Analytical chemist, 344

Ancient bacteria, *c*11

Anemometer, 179, *c*195

Aneroid barometer, *c*194

Animals

adaptations of, 26–29

and balance in ecosystem, 112–113

bioluminescence of, 416

building blocks of, 6

cells, 8

classifying, 18–25

energy in, 84

fossils, *c*244

genus, 12

instincts, 30–31, *c*31

invertebrates, 22–25

kingdom, *c*11, *c*13

learning behaviors, *c*32, *c*33

living side by side, 116

natural resources for, 287

needs of, 111

as parasites, *c*117

seeds and, 60, *c*61

symmetry of, *c*36–*c*37

vertebrates, 18–21

Anther, 55

Antibodies, 161

Appalachian Mountains, 117

Apple trees, 65

Archimedes, 480

Archimedes' Screw, 480

Arctic Ocean, *c*183

Armstrong, Neil, 525

Arteries in heart, *c*151

Arthropods, 22

Art in Science 19, 29, 55, 89, 119, 127, 191, 249, 267, 319, 381, 417, 529

Ash (volcanic), 273, *c*273

Asian long-horned beetle, *p*117

Asteroid belt, 520, c520
Asteroids, 520
Astronauts, c446
    ecosystem for, 102–103
Astronomy, 514, 519
Atlantic Ocean, c183, p184
Atmosphere
    of Earth, 183, 188, 524
    of Jupiter, 528, c528
    of Mars, 527
    of Mercury, 522
    of the Moon, 524
    of Neptune, p534
    of Pluto, 536
    of Uranus, 532
    of Venus, 523
Atoms, 375, 378
Atrium, 150
Attraction in objects, 376
Auger, p471
Aurora borealis (northern lights), p385
Auto engineer, 304
Automobile mass production, c558
Avalanches and gravity, 268
Axis, p490, 493, 496, 499

Bacteria, p158, p159
Balance, 485
    in ecosystems, 111–113
    people and, 124–129
Balanced forces, 444
Ball-and-socket joints, c144
Bar graphs, 68
Bar magnet, c383
Barometer, p179, 194, p194

Barriers
    to animal migration, 30
    to control erosion, c269
Basalt, p246
Bats, p56, 405
Beak of birds, 26
Bedrock, p289
Bees, 56, p56
Behaviors of animals
    by instinct, 30–31, c31
    learned, 32–33, p32, p33
    partly inherited and partly learned, 33
Bifocal glasses, c425
Biography
    Archimedes, 480
    Otis Boykin, 568
    Rachel Carson, 104
    Rebecca J. Cole, 168
    Nicolaus Copernicus, 544
    Rebecca Lee Crumpler, 168
    Joseph B. Duckworth, 232
    William Gilbert, 400
    Robert B. Lee III, 512
    Doug Ming, p256
    Max Planck, 368
    Joanne Simpson, 208
Biologists
    animal, 40
    plant, 40, 72
    wildlife, 40
Bioluminescence, 416
Birds
    adaptations by, 26, p28
    beak of, 26
    characteristics of, c18
Black holes, p419
Black smokers (hot springs), 280

Blacktailed jackrabbit, p85, c88
Blending, 28, p28
Block and tackle pulley, p467
Blood cells, 161
Blood circulation, 150, c151
Body temperature of reptiles, p18
Boiling point, 335
Bones, 140, 144, 145, c145
Boykin, Otis, 568
Brain, 154, c155
Bricks, p291
Bristlecone pine trees, 58
Bronchial tube, 148, c149
Buds, 64, c65
Building blocks See Cell
Bulbs, 64, c64
Burmese python, 20, c20–c21
Burning wood, p336

Calcite, 239, c241
Calcium, 144
Callisto (moon), p529
Canada geese, 30, p30
Can opener, 472, c472
Carbon dioxide
    in atmosphere, 188
    in circulatory system, 150, c151
    as greenhouse gas, 199
    for plants, 48
    released by organisms, c94
    in respiratory system, 148
    weathering by, 265
Cardiac muscle, c147

Career
Analytical Chemist, 344
Auto Engineer, 304
Biologist, 40
Ecologist, 136
Oceanographer, 280
Optometrist, 432
Plant Biologist, 72, p72
Space Engineer, 456

Carnivores, p74, 84, c85, 90

Carson, Rachel, 104, p104

Cartilage, 148

Cassiopeia (constellation), c504, c505

Cause and Effect, 109, 115, 121, 135, 181, 185, 189, 193, 285, 291, 295, 303, 349, 353, 359, 364, 373, 379, 389, 399, 493, 499, 505, 511

Cell, 7
of onion, 5
parts of, 8
plant, 47, 50

Cell body in neuron, 154

Cell membrane, 8, c8, c49

Cell wall, 9

Celsius temperature scale, 352, c352, c362, 362–363

Cenozoic Era, c245

Central nervous system, 154, c155

Change of State, 320

Chapter Review and Test Prep, 38–39, 70–71, 100–101, 134–135, 166–167, 204–205, 230–231, 254–255, 278–279, 302–303, 342–343, 364–365, 398–399, 430–431, 454–455, 478–479, 510–511, 542–543, 564–565

Charged objects. See Electrically charged objects

Charged particles and auroras, 385, p385

Charon (Pluto's moon), 536, p536

Chemical change, p315, 336, p336

Chemical water pollution, 125

Chemical weathering, 265

Chicken pox, 161

Chlorophyll, c43, 49

Chloroplasts, c3, 9, 49, c49

Circle graph, c300, 300–301

Circuit, 378
closed, c379
parallel, 381, c381
series, 380, c380

Circulatory system, 150, c151

Cirrus clouds, c192, c193

Class (animal kingdom), c13

Classification systems
animal kingdom, c13
kingdoms, 10, c11
smaller groups, 12

Classify, 2
animals, 18–25
plants, 14–17
tornadoes, 224, c224

Classifying, 34, 35, c35, 38, 100, 236, 278, 342, 455, 478

Clay, 90, 267, 290–291, p290–p291

Clean Water Act, 125

Clermont (steamboat), c558

Climate, 119, 198

Closed circuit, c379

Clothing
plant fibers for, 63
from polyester, 552

Clouds
cold front and, 191
formation and types of, 193, c193
of Venus, 523
warm front and, c192

Clue words, 77, 261, 285, 317, 373

Coal, 294, c294
land reclamation and, 127
strip mining, 126–127

Cold front, 191, c191

Colds (disease), 158, p159

Cole, Rebecca J., 168

Collecting Data, 108, 130, 131, 302, 338, 339, 450

Colors
as animal adaptation, 28
light and, 420, c420
of minerals, 240
in visible spectrum, 418, c418, c419

Columbus, Christopher, 384

Communicating, 174, 180, 204, 311, 460, 475, 487, 575

Communication, 546
methods of, 556, c556
telecommunications, 557, c557

Community, p74, c83
changes in environment and, c118–c119
of ecosystem, 82
succession and, 118–119

Compare and Contrast, 5, 9, 17, 25, 39, 261, 265, 269, 279, 317, 321, 337, 343

Compass, 384, c384

Competition, c106, 114

Complex machines, 472–473, c472, c473

Compound lens, c425

Compound pulley, c467

Compression, p402, 408

Computers

for predicting hurricanes, 220

transportation systems and, 559

Concave lenses, 424, c424

Conclusions. *See* Draw Conclusions

Condensation, 178, c186, 187, 335

Conduction, c347, 358, c359

Conductors, c346, c355, 378

Cones of conifers, 16

Conglomerate, c242

Conifers, c16, 54

Conservation, c283, c296

Constellations, 491, 504–505, c504, c505

Consumers

in ecosystem, 84

of Sonoran Desert, c85

Contact lenses, c425

Convection, 356, c357, 358

conduction, radiation, and, c359

radiators and, 357

Convection current, c347, 356

Convex lenses, c424

Cooking with solar energy, 367

Copernicus, Nicolaus, 530, 544

Coral reefs, p91

Corundum crystals, 239

Coughing, c157

Coyote, 86, c87, 88, c89

Crater of volcano, 270

Craters, 514, 526

on Mercury, 522

on the Moon, 524

Crescent Moon, c501

Cross Curricular links

Art in Science, 19, 29, 55, 89, 119, 127, 191, 249, 267, 319, 381, 417, 529

Health in Science, 51, 155, 409, 503

Math in Science, 7, 15, 23, 27, 36–37, 47, 59, 81, 84, 113, 145, 149, 150, 164–165, 183, 197, 219, 228–229, 247, 252–253, 300–301, 323, 325, 333, 356, 387, 391, 393, 396–397, 421, 423, 428–429, 447, 452–453, 463, 465, 501, 508–509, 523, 533, 535, 537, 540–541, 562–563

Social Studies in Science, 11, 31, 63, 83, 90, 117, 129, 143, 159, 195, 215, 217, 271, 289, 331, 355, 375, 383, 413, 469, 495, 519, 557

Technology in Science, 33, 125, 161, 187, 327, 389, 449

Writing in Science, 13, 21, 39, 53, 57, 61, 71, 79, 93, 101, 111, 123, 135, 153, 167, 199, 205, 223, 231, 255, 263, 273, 279, 287, 293, 297, 303, 329, 335, 343, 351, 365, 377, 385, 399, 407, 431, 441, 445, 455, 471, 497, 511, 521, 525, 531, 543, 551, 555, 565

Crowding, 108

Crumb rubber, p296

Crumpler, Rebecca Lee, 168

Crust of Earth, 263, 272

Crystals in minerals, 239

Cumulonimbus clouds, c193

Cumulus clouds, c192, 193, c193

Cuyahoga River, 125, p125

Cytoplasm, 3, 8, p8, p9

D

Dandelions, 10, c10, 47

Daylight, c497, c508, 508–509

DDT, 104

Decay

carbon dioxide and, 94, c94, p95

in ecosystems, 94, c94

moisture and, 94

oxygen and, 94, c94

rate of, 94

Decimals (decimal number), 276, c340

Decomposers, 75, 96–97

decay and, 94

in ecosystem, 87

Deer, 84, 115

Degrees Celsius. *See* Celsius temperature scale

Degrees Fahrenheit. *See* Fahrenheit temperature scale

Delta, 267

Density, 314, 326, c326

comparing densities, 327, p327, c340, 340–341

finding, 326

Deposition, 259, 261, 267
    controlling, 269
    soil renewal and, 288
Desalinators, 187
Desert, 80, p80
    deposition in, 267
    food chain in, 86
    food web in, 88, c88–c89
Desert bighorn sheep, c82, c83, c88
Diaphragm, 148, c149
Digestion, 152, c153
Directed Inquiry, Explore, 4, 44, 76, 108, 140, 180, 212, 236, 260, 284, 316, 348, 372, 404, 436, 460, 492, 516, 548
Discovery Videos, 73, 233, 369, 513
Disease, 162–163
Distance, 452–453, 463
Doorbell, 388, c388
Doorknob, 466, p466
Doppler radar, 224, c224, p224
Dormant, 43, 62
Dormant volcano, 271
Draw Conclusions, 45, 49, 65, 71, 141, 147, 157, 167, 405, 411, 415, 419, 425, 431
Dreschel, Tom, p72
Ducks, 26, c26
Duckworth, Joseph B., 232
Dust devil, p223
Dust storms on Mars, 527
Dynamo, 391

Ear, 415, c415
Earphones, 388, c389
Earth, c183, 183, 494, 495, c520, p524, c524
    atmosphere, 188
    axis, c498–499, 499
    crust of, 198, 263
    geologic time periods, c245
    landforms, 263
    lunar eclipse and, 502, c502
    as magnet, 384
    mass, 446
    Moon, Sun, and, 500
    motion, 495
    moving plates, c272, 272
    revolution, 493, c498
    rotation, 496
    solar eclipse and, c503, 503
    volcanoes and, c270, 270, c271, 271
    water on, 183–185, c184, c185
    weathering and, 264–265
Earth Observing System (EOS), 206–207
Earthquakes, 259, 272, c272
    comparing sizes of, c276, 276–277
    effects of, 273, p273
Earthquake scale, 276
Earthworms, 76
Echoes, 411
Eclipse, 490, 502
    lunar, 502, c502
    solar, 503, c503
E. coli, p158
Ecologist, 136

Ecosystems, 73–104
    balance in, 111–113
    change in, 105–136, 114
    community in, 82
    competition in, 114
    consumers in, 84, c85, 87
    decay in, 94
    decomposers in, 87
    energy flow, 84–87
    environment and, c118–c119, 118–123
    fires in, c122–c123
    flow of matter, 90–95
    food web in, 88–89, c88–c89
    habitat in, 82
    human activities and, 124–129
    kinds of, c80–c81
    land pollution in, 126
    land reclamation in, 127
    living and nonliving parts of, 79
    niche in, 82
    organisms in, 114–117
    parts of, 79–83
    population of, 82, c98, 98–99
    producers in, 84, 86
    in space, 102–103
    succession in, 118, 119, c118–119
    systems and, 79
Edison, Thomas, c392, 417
Effort, 458, 464, c464, 465, c465
Eggbeater, c473
Eggs
    of snails, 24, c25
    of snakes, c20
Einstein, Albert, 368

Electrically charged objects, *p*376

Electrical Safety Foundation, 393

Electric charges, 375

   flow of, 378–379, *c*379

   number line to represent, *c*396, 396–397

Electric current, 370, 378, 391

   light bulb and, 417

   in parallel circuit, 381

   in series circuit, 380

Electric field, 377

Electricity (electrical energy)

   circuits, 378, *c*379, 380–381, *c*380–*c*381

   discoveries in, *c*392

   energy from flowing water and, 293

   from generators, 391

   magnetism and, 386–389, 390–391

   model of circuit, 378, *c*379

   movement of, 378–379, *c*379

   safe use of, 393

   from solar energy, *c*292, 293

   static, 375

Electric motor, *c*388–*c*389, 391

Electric telegraph, *c*557

Electric trolley streetcars, *c*558

Electromagnet, 371, *c*386, 386–387, *c*387, *c*388–*c*389

Electromagnetic radiation, 418

Electromagnetic spectrum, 418, *p*419

Electromagnetic waves, 418, *p*419

Element, 337, *c*337

Ellipse, 491, 498, *c*498

Elliptical orbits, 521

Email, 556

Endangered species, 107, 120

Energy. *See also* Solar energy

   changing types of, *c*449

   in closed circuit, *c*379

   flow in food chain, 86

   kinetic (motion), 448

   in matter, 351

   methods of conservation, 296

   nonrenewable sources of, 294–295

   phase changes and, 334

   in plants and animals, 84

   potential (stored), 448

   renewable sources of, 292–293

   thermal, 351

   transfer, 86

Energy Department's American Solar Challenge, 304

Environment, *c*118–*c*119, 118–123

   fossils and, 121

   human activities and, 124–129

   organisms and, 82

   plant growth and, 130–131, *c*131

   plants and animals in, 80–81

   preservation of, 128–129

   technology and, 554

Epicenter, 259, 272, *c*272

Equator, 495, 499

Erosion, 242, 259, 261, 266

   controlling, 269

   soil renewal and, 288

Eruptions of volcanoes, 270, *c*270, *p*271

Esophagus, *c*153

Estimating and Measuring 201, 284, 308, 310, 360, 484, 516, 574

Euglena, *p*84

Europa (moon), *c*529

Evaporation, 178, *c*186, *p*329

Everglades National Park, 90, *p*91, *p*129

Evergreen plants, *c*16

Exoskeleton of arthropods, 22

Experiment. *See* Full Inquiry, Experiment

Explore. *See* Directed Inquiry, Explore

Extinct, *p*107

Eyeglasses, *c*424

Eye of human. *See* Human eye

Eye of hurricane, *c*217, 232

F

Fahrenheit temperature scale, *c*352, *c*362, 362–363

Fall (season), 499

Family in animal kingdom, *c*13

Faraday, Michael, *p*391, *c*392

Fault, *c*259, 272, *c*272

Feathers, 26

Feldspar, *p*239, 240

***Felis* genus,** 12

Fern spores, *c*16

Fertilization

   changes after, 57

   by plants, *c*43, 56, *c*56

Fertilizers, 555

Fibrous roots, 52, *c*52

Fins, 29

Fire
from earthquakes, *c*273
in ecosystems, *c*122–*c*123
as light source, 416
Firefly, *p*416
Fish, *c*18, 27, *p*28, 29
Flashlight, 391
Fleming, Alexander, *c*160
Floating and density, 326–327, 340, 341
Floods, 123, 219
Flowering plant, 54
life cycle of, *c*58–*c*59
seeds from, *c*16
Flowers
incomplete, *c*55
parts of, *c*42, *c*54–*c*55
Flute, *c*413
Food
in digestive system, 152, *c*153
how plants make food, 48–49
need for, 111
plant leaves and, *c*50
technology and, 554
Food chain, 86
Food poisoning, *p*158
Food web, *c*88–*c*89, *c*92–*c*93
Force, 434
balanced, 444
combining, *c*443
friction as, 445
gravity as, 446
mass and, 444
measuring, 447
motion and, *c*442, 444
moving objects and, 442–443

Ford, Henry, *c*558
Forde, Evan B., *p*280
Forecasting tornadoes, *c*224
Forest, *p*80, 286
Forest fires, *c*122–*c*123
Forming Questions and Hypotheses, 172, 231, 308, 398, 484, 510, 572,
Fossil fuels, *c*282
climate changes and, 199
forming, 294, 298–299
impact of, 295
Fossils
of ancient species, *c*121
formation of, 245
information from, *c*244
Fractions, 132
Frame of reference, 434, *c*440
Franklin, Benjamin, 375, *c*392, *c*425
Fraunhofer, Joseph von, *c*425
Frequency, *c*402, *c*409
Freshwater ecosystem, *c*91
Freshwater snail, *p*90, *c*92
Friction, 434, 468–469
Frogs, 29
Front, 178, 190
Fruits, 57
Fujita Scale, *c*224
Fujita, T. Theodore, 224
Fulcrum, 458, *c*464, *c*465
Full Inquiry, Experiment, 172–175, 308–311, 484–487, 572–575
Full Moon, 501, *c*501
Fulton, Robert, *c*558
Fungi, *c*11, 116

Gabbro, *p*247
Gagarin, Yuri, 525
Galaxy, 514, *p*518, 519
Galena, *p*240
Galileo, 400, *c*424, *p*530
Galileo's Handles, 530
Galle, Johann, 535
Galveston, Texas, hurricane, 219
Gamma rays, *c*419
Ganymede (moon), *c*529
Garbage
land pollution and, 126
recycling of, *c*132, 132–133
Garden hose reel, 466, *p*466
Gas (state of matter), 320, *c*321
light traveling through, 422
sound waves in, 410, *c*410
Gears, 472
Generator (electric), 391, *c*392, 393, *c*393
Genus, *p*2, 12, *c*13
Geologic time scale, 245, *c*245
Germination of spore, 62
Geysers, 128
Giant's Causeway, 247, *p*247
Gilbert, William, 384, *c*392, 400
Glaciers, 183, *p*184, 185
climate information from, 198
erosion by, 266
Glass recycling, 297, *c*297
Global warming, 295
Gneiss, *p*248

Graduated cylinder, 325, c325

Grafting of plants, 65

Gram (g), 323

Gramme, Zenobe, c392

Granite, 239, p239, p247

Graph

bar, c411

circle, c300, 300–301

Graphic Organizer, c5, c9, c45, c77, c109, c141, c181, c207, c213, c237, c261, c285, c317, c349, c373, c405, c437, c461, c510

Grassland, p80

Gravity, 434, 446

air pressure and, 188, c189

avalanches and, 268

between Earth and Sun, 498

landslides and, 268

moons and, 524

planets, orbits, and, 520

Great Red Spot (Jupiter), c528

Great Smoky Mountains, c113

Greenhouse gases, 199

Groups for protection, 115

Guided Inquiry Investigate, 34–35, 66–67, 96–97, 130–131, 162–163, 200–201, 226–227, 250–251, 274–275, 298–299, 338–339, 360–361, 394–395, 426–427, 450–451, 474–475, 506–507, 538–539, 560–561

Guitar, c414

Gutenberg, Johann, c556

Habitats, 82, c83

Halibut, 27

Halley, Edmund, 517

Halley's Comet, 517

Hawks, 115

Hazardous waste, p106, 126

Health

keeping human body healthy, 158

and technology, 552, c553

Health in Science, 51, 155, 409, 503

Hearing, 415, c415

Heart, c8, 150, c151

Heat, c351. *See also* Thermal energy

conduction and, c354

convection and, 356, c357

radiation and, c358

vs. temperature, 353

Heat transfer, 349, 367

Helmet, 552, c553

Henry, Joseph, p391, c392

Herbivores, p74, 84, c85, 90

Hernandez, Estela, p456

Hertz, 409

Hibernation, 30, c31

High-energy waves, 418

Highway travel time, c453

Hinge joint, 144, c144

Hornblende, c241

Horseshoe magnet, c382

Host, 117, c117

Hot-air balloons, 349

House cat, 12, p12

How to Read Science, xx, xxi, 5, 45, 77, 109, 141, 181, 213, 237, 261, 285, 317, 349, 373, 405, 437, 461, 493, 517, 549; *See also* Target Reading Skills

Hubble Space Telescope, c536

Human

adaptations of, 27

behavior of, 33

Human body

bacteria, viruses, and, c158, c159

central nervous system of, 154, c155

circulatory system of, 150, c151

defenses of, 156, c157

digestive system of, 152–153, c153

immune system of, 161

infectious disease and, c158–c159, c160

microorganisms in, 156

muscular system of, c146, c147

organ systems of, 143

respiratory system of, 148, c149

skeletal system of, 144, c145

units of measure and, c164, c165

vaccines and, 161

Human eye, c422, 432

Humidity, 178, 195, c195

Humus, p283, 289

Hurricane, 210, 214, 215

compared to tornado, 225

eye of, c217, 232

formation of, c216

names of, c219

predicting, c220

Saffir-Simpson scale for rating, 228

as system, 217

winds and water of, c218, 218–219

Hurricane Andrew, 213, 215, p219

Hurricane models, 221, c221

Hydroelectric power, c393

Hygrometer, 195, c195

Ice, 183, 264, 266, 321

Ice Man, p152

Identifying and Controlling Variables, 172, 308, 572

Igneous rocks, p235, p246, p247, c249

Immune system, p139, 161

Inclined plane, 458, c468, c469

Incomplete flowers, 55, c55

Indian Ocean, c183, c184

Inertia, 444

Infectious disease, p138, 158, c160

Inferring, 38, 66, 67, 70, 96, 97, 100, 131, 134, 140, 162, 163, 166, 204, 226, 230, 254, 260, 274, 275, 278, 284, 299, 316, 342, 348, 364, 372, 395, 398, 404, 426, 427, 454, 478, 510, 539, 542, 548, 560, 561

Influenza, c159

In-line skates, 552, p552, c553

Insects, 28, p28

Instincts, 30–31, c31

Instruments. See Musical instruments

Insulated wire, c379

Insulator, p346, 355, p355, 378

International Bird and Rescue Research Center, 125

Internet, 4, 68, 98, 132, 204, 276, 300, 337, 452, 462

Interpreting Data, 200, 201, 204, 431, 436, 451

Intestines, 152, c153

Invertebrates, p3, 22, c22, 22–25, c23, c24, c25

Investigate. See Guided Inquiry, Investigate

Investigating and Experimenting, 308, 339, 398, 474, 484, 572

Involuntary muscles, 139, 146, 147, c147

Io (moon), c529

Iron oxide on Mars, 526

Jackson, Dionne Broxton, p343

Jenner, Edward, c160

Jet engine, c559

Joints, 144, c144

Jupiter, 385, 520, c520, 528, p528, c528, 529, c529

Journal. See Science Journal

Kepler, Johannes, 400

Key Biscayne lighthouse, p219

Keyhole surgery, 554

Kilauea (volcano), 271

Kilogram (kg), 323

Kinetic energy, 434, 448, 449, c449

Kingdoms, 10

    ancient bacteria, 11, c11

    animals, 11, c11

    fungi, 11, c11

    plants, 11, c11

    protists, 11, c11

    true bacteria, 11, c11

Kinnersley, Ebenezer, c392

Koch, Robert, c160

Krakatau (volcano), 273

Lab report, 317

Lab Zone

    4, 34–35, 37, 40, 44, 66–67, 69, 72, 76, 96–97, 99, 103, 104, 108, 130–131, 133, 136, 140, 162–163, 165, 168, 172–175, 180, 200–201, 203, 207, 208, 212, 226–227, 229, 232, 236, 250–251, 253, 256, 260, 274–275, 277, 280, 284, 298–299, 301, 304, 308–311, 316, 338–339, 341, 344, 348, 360–361, 363, 367, 368, 372, 394–395, 397, 400, 404, 426–427, 429, 432, 436, 450–451, 453, 456, 460, 474–475, 477, 480, 484–487, 492, 506–507, 509, 512, 516, 538–539, 541, 544, 548, 560–561, 563, 567, 572–575; See also Activities

Lakes, 183, c184, 185

Land, 126, p126

Land breeze, 188

Landfills, 126, p126, 132

Landforms, c258, 263

    deposition and, 267, 269

    erosion and, 266, 269

    gravity and, 268

    volcanoes, c270, 270–271, c271

    weathering and, 264–265

Land pollution, 126

Land reclamation, 127, c127

Landslide, p258, 259, 268, p268

Language, 33

Large intestine, c153

Lasers, 425, p425

Lava, 246, 270

Lawn mower, c473

Learning, 32–33, c32–c33

Leaves, c34–c35, 47, p47, c50–c51

   cross-section of, c48

   stoma of, c48, c51

   sunlight and arrangement of, 51, c51

Lee, Robert B. III, 512, p512

Leeuwenhoek, Anton van, 7, c425

Length, c324

Lenses, 424, c424

Lever, 458, 464, c464

   formula for, 464

   groups of, 465, c465

Leverrier, Urbain, 535

Lichen, 116, p116, 124

Life cycle

   of brown garden snail, 24–25, c24–c25

   of plant, c58–c59, 58–65, c62, c64–c65

   of reptile, 20–21, c20–c21

Life jacket, p327

Light

   color and, p420

   fiber optics and, 425

   human eye and, c422

   lasers and, 425

   lenses and, 424

   matter and, 420

   opaque materials and, 421

   for plants, p44

   refraction of, 422

   shadows and, 417

   sources of, 416

   translucent materials and, 421

   transparent materials and, 421

Light bulb, 417, p417

Lightning, 374, p374, 375

Light wave, 418

   absorption and, c421

   reflection and, c421

Limestone, p243

Line graphs, 204

Line of symmetry, c36–c37

Linnaeus, Carolus, 11

Liquid, 320–321, p321

   light in, 422

   sound waves in, 410, c410

Lister, Joseph, 159

Liter (L), 325

Living space, 111, 114

Living things, 4, 111. See also Animal; Human; Plant

Load, 458, 464–465, c464–c465

Lodestone, 382

Longitudinal waves, 408

Lumber, 63

Lunar eclipse, 490, 502, c502

Lungs, 18, 19, 148, c149

Luster of minerals, p235, 240, c240

Machines, p462, 463. See also Complex machines; Simple machines

Maglev rail system, c559

Magma, 246, c249, 270, p526

Magnesia, 382

Magnet, 382, c442

   Earth as, 384

   separating mixtures using, p328, 329

Magnetic field, 370, 382

Magnetic north pole, 384, c385

Magnetic poles, c382–c383

Magnetic resonance imaging (MRI), 549

Magnetic south pole, 384, c385

Magnetism, 370, 382, 400, c442

   electricity transformed to, 386–389

   of Sun, 521

   transforming to electricity, 390–391

Magnitude of earthquake, 276

Main Idea and Details, 213, 221, 225, 231, 549, 553, 559, 565

Making and Using Models, 162, 163, 212, 231, 298, 299, 364, 516, 538, 539, 548, 561, 564

Making Operational Definitions, 394, 395

Mammals

   adaptations of, c27

   characteristics of, c18

   hibernation by, c31

Map as scale drawing, 564

Marble, 355, c355

Marco Polo, c424

Marine creature fossils, 121

Markings (animal), c28

Mars, 520, c520, 526–527, p526, c526–c527

Mars Exploration Rovers, c527

Mars Pathfinder, 366, 527

Marshes, 90

Mass, 322
- force and, 444
- friction and, 445
- gravity and, 446
- motion and, 484–487
- weight and, 446

Math in Science
- 7, 15, 23, 27, 36–37, 47, 59, 68–69, 81, 84, 98–99, 113, 132–133, 145, 149, 150, 164–165, 183, 197, 204–205, 219, 228–229, 247, 252–253, 300–301, 323, 325, 333, 340–341, 356, 387, 391, 393, 396–397, 421, 423, 428–429, 447, 452–453, 463, 465, 476–477, 501, 508–509, 523, 533, 535, 537, 540–541, 562–563

Matter
- charging, 375–377
- chemical changes in, 336
- density of, c326, 340–341
- elements and Periodic Table, c337
- energy in, 351
- gases, c321
- heat and temperature of, 353
- liquids, c321
- mass of, 322
- measuring, 322–327
- metric units to measure and compare, 323, c323
- mixtures and, 328–329
- phase changes in, 334–335
- physical changes in, 332–333
- properties of, 319
- solids, c321
- solubility and, c331
- solutions and, c330
- states of, 320
- temperature and, c334–c335
- testing, 319
- volume of, 324–325

Mauna Loa, 247

Measurement
- of force, 447
- of human body, c164–c165
- of matter, 322–327, p324
- of weather, c194, c195

Medical technology
- improved care and, 554
- NMR and MRI, 555
- pacemaker, 568
- x-rays, c555

Melting point, 335

Mercury, c520, p522

Mercury barometer, c194

Mesozoic Era, c245

Metals
- as conductor, 355, c355
- used by NASA, 343

Metamorphic rocks, p235, p248, c249

Meteorites, 524

Meteorologists, 178, 194
- Joanne Simpson, 208
- predicting hurricanes, 220, c220

Metric lengths, c325

Metric system, 323–324, c323–c324

Mica, p239, 240

Microorganisms, c156–c157, c160

Microscope, p7, c425
- bamboo stem and, c14
- onion cells and, 5
- plant cells and, 47

Microwaves, 418, c418

Midnight Sun, c499

Migration, 30, p30

Milky Way, 518, p518

Millibars (mb), 194

Milligram (mg), 323

Milliliter (mL), 325

Mineral, p234, p239
- identifying, c240, c241
- nutrients for plants, 47
- rock-forming, 239
- for strong bones, 144
- wearing away, 260

Ming, Douglas, 256, p256

Mining
- coal, 126, 127
- fossil fuels, c295
- land reclamation and, 127

Mission to Planet Earth (NASA), 367

Mistletoe, p117

Mixture, p314, c328, 328–329, c329

Mohs Scale for Hardness, c240

Moisture and decay, 94

Mollusk, 22, p24, c25

Monkeys, 33, c33

Moon (of Earth), 524
- Earth, Sun, and, 500
- exploration of, 256, p525
- lunar eclipse and, c502
- mass of, 446
- orbit and rotation of, c500
- phases of, c501
- solar eclipse and, c503

Moons, 524
- of Jupiter, c529

of Mars, 526

of Neptune, 535

of Saturn, c531

of Uranus, c533

Mosses, p15

and oak trees, 116

reproduction cycle of, 62

Spanish, p52

sphagnum, 63

spores from, 16

Motion, c440

energy of, 448–449

force and, 442–444, c442–c443

friction and, 445

measuring, 440–441

relative, 439

speed and, 440, c441

types of, 439

velocity and, c441

Motion picture cameras, c557

Mountain, p262, 263, 268

Mountain lion, 84, p85

in food web, 88, c89

scientific name of, 12, p12

Mount Kenya (volcano), 271

Mount Pinatubo (volcano), 273

Mount Rainier (volcano), 271

Mount St. Helens (volcano), p271

Mount Tambora (volcano), 273

Mouth, p153

MRI (magnetic resonance imaging), 555

Mucus, 156, c157

Mudslides, 219

Mudstone, 243, p243

Multicelled organisms, 47

Muscles, c146–c147

involuntary, 146

skeleton and, 144

tissue, 147, c147

voluntary, 146

Muscular system, c146, c147

Mushrooms, p10, p110

Musical instruments, c413–c415

Nail, c470

Names

of living things, 12

of storms, 219, c219

NASA (National Aeronautics and Space Administration),

Analytical Chemist, 344

Biologist, 40

Cooking in the Sun, 366–367

Ecologist, 136

Ecosystems in Space, 102–103

Eye in the Sky, 206–207

Robert B. Lee III, 512

Doug Ming, 256

Plant Biologist, 72

Space Engineer, 456

Telemedicine, 566–567

Weather Modification Pilot, 208

National Oceanic and Atmospheric Administration (NOAA), p280

National Park system, 128–129

National Weather Service

storm names of, c219

tornado watches and warnings from, 225

Natural events, 122

Natural resource. *See also*

Nonrenewable energy sources; Renewable natural resources

competition for, 114

conservation of, 296

ecosystem populations and changes in, 114

recycling and, c296, c297

sharing, 115

use of, 287

Nectar, 56

Needles of pine trees, 50

Needs of living things, 111

Negative charge (–), 375–376

Negative electric field, 377

Neptune, c520, p534, c534

Neuron, p138, c154

Neutral objects, 375–376

New Moon, c501

Newton (unit of force), 447

Newton, Isaac, c424, 447

Niche in habitat, 82

Nightingale, Florence, c160

Nimbo, 193

Nitrogen in atmosphere, 188

NMR technology, 555

Noise pollution, 413

Nonrenewable energy sources, 294

conservation of, 296, p296

fossil fuels, 294–295

Nonvascular plants, c15

Northern Hemisphere

hours of daylight throughout the year for, c497

midnight Sun and, c499

tilted toward Sun, c499

Northern lights, p385

North Pole, c498

North-seeking pole, p383

North Star, 505

Nuclear energy, 393

Nucleus, *p*2, 8, *c*8

Number line

to compare densities, *c*340

for electrical charges, *c*396, 396–397

Internet, 396

Nutrients

in digestive system, 152, *c*153

in plants, 14–15

Oak trees, 116

Observing, 4, 44, 66, 67, 70, 76, 96, 97, 108, 130, 131, 134, 163, 174, 236, 250, 251, 260, 274, 275, 302, 310, 316, 338, 339, 343, 348, 372, 394, 404, 426, 450, 485, 492, 506, 507, 560, 561

Obsidian, *p*246

Oceanographer, 280

Oceans, 183, *p*184

ecosystems in, *c*91

pollution in, 125

saltiness of, 184–185

solutions in, 330

studying with sound waves, 411

Oersted, Hans Christian, 386, *c*392

O'Hair, Ralph, 232

Oil, 125, 294

Oil rigs, *p*295

Oil spills, 295

Okefenokee National Wildlife Refuge, *p*129

Okefenokee Swamp, 90, *p*91, 92

Old Man of the Mountain (New Hampshire), *p*264

Omnivores, *p*74, 84, *c*85, 86

One-celled organisms, *c*11, *c*84

Onion, *p*5, 64

Opaque, *p*402, 421

Optical Fibers, 425, *c*425, 546, 554

Optometrist, 432

Orbit, 490, *c*498

elliptical, 520

of moons (satellites), 524

of Neptune, 534

of planets, 520

of Pluto, 537

Order (animal kingdom), *c*13

Ore, *p*282, 294

Oregon Trail, *c*453

Organ, *c*8, 143

Organ systems, *c*8, *p*143

central nervous system, 154, *c*155

circulatory system, 150, *c*151

digestive system, 152–153, *c*153

muscular system, *c*146, *c*147

respiratory system, 148, *c*149

skeletal system, 144, *c*145

Organisms, *c*8

balance of ecosystem and, 112–113

as consumers, 84

naming of, 12

one-celled, *c*11

relationships in ecosystems, 114–117

Orion (constellation), *c*505

Orpiment, *p*240

Outer space

black holes in, *c*419

vacuum in, 410

Ovary, *p*43, *c*57

pistil, 56

pollination, 57

Oxygen

in atmosphere, 188

in circulatory system, 150, *c*151

decay and, 94–95, *c*95

as natural resource, 287

as photosynthesis waste, 47

in respiratory system, 148

Pacemaker, *c*568

Pacific Ocean, *c*183–*c*184

Paleozoic Era, *c*245

Pan balance, 322–323

Paper, 291

as plant product, 63

recycling of, 297, *c*297

Parallel circuit, 370, *c*381

Parasite, *p*107, *c*117

Parents, *c*32

Parsons, Charles, *c*392

Particles

in atoms, 375

charged, 375

heat and temperature of, 353

in matter, 320, *c*321

thermal energy and, 351

Passenger pigeon, 120, *p*120

Pasteur, Louis, *c*160

Pathogens, *p*138, 158, *c*160, 162–163, *c*163

Peat, 63

Pegmatite, *p247*

Penicillin, *c160*

Peninsulas, 263

Percussion instrument, *c413*, 414

Periodic Table, *c337*

Pesticides, 555

Petals, *c54*, 55, 57

Petroleum, *p282*, 294

Petunias, *c68*, 68–69

Pharynx, 148, *c149*

Phase changes, *c334–c335*

Phases of the Moon, *c501*

Phobos (moon), 526

Photosynthesis, *p42*, *c47*

    carbon dioxide and oxygen during, 95

    sunlight energy and, 84

Phyllite, *p248*

Phylum (animal kingdom), *c13*

Physical change, *p314*, *c332–c335*

Physical weathering, 264

Physicians

    Cole, Rebecca J., 168, *p168*

    Crumpler, Rebecca Lee, 168, *p168*

Physicist, 368

Piano, *c414–c415*

Pine trees, 50

Pistil, *p42*, *c54*, 55, 56, *c57*

Plains, 263

Planck, Max, 368

Planets

    diameters of, *c540*, 540–541

    inner, *c520*, *c522–c527*

    outer, *c520*, *c528–c537*

    Sedna as, *p537*

    in solar system, *c520*

Plant

    and balance in ecosystem, 112–113

    building blocks of, 6

    cells of, 8, *c9*

    characteristics of, 47–49

    chloroplasts of, 48, *c48*

    classifying, 14–17

    energy in, 84

    environment and growth of, 130–131, *c131*

    flowers of, 54–55, *c54–c55*

    food made by, 47–48, *c47–c48*

    fossils of, 244–245

    grafting, 65

    growing without seed, 66–67

    habitats of, 47

    kingdom, *c11*, 47

    leaves of, *c47–c48*, *c50–c51*

    life cycle of, *c58–c65*

    natural resources for, 287

    needs of, 111

    nonvascular, *c15*

    as parasites, *c117*

    parts of, *c50–c53*

    photosynthesis, *c47*

    pollen and fertilization of, 56

    reproduction by, *c16–c17*, *c54–c57*

    roots of, 52–53

    spores, *c16*

    stems of, *c47*, *c51*

    sunlight and, *c68*, 68–69, 416

    transpiration and, *c51*

    uses of, 63

    vascular, 14

    weathering by, 264–265

Plant biologists, 40, 72, *p72*

Plant cells, 47

Plantlike protist, *p84*, *p90*

Plastic

    as insulator, *c355*

    recycling of, *p296*

Plateaus, 263

Plates (of Earth), *c272*

Pluto, *c520*, *p536*, *c536–c537*

Poison, 29

Polar ice caps, 183, *c184*, 185

Poles of magnet. *See* Magnetic poles

Pollen, *c54*, 55–56, *c57*

Pollination, *c56–c57*

Pollution, 124

Polyester, 552

Polyurethane, *c553*

Populations, *p75*, *c83*

    ecosystems and, *c82*, 114

    of endangered and threatened species, *c120*

    of extinct species, *c120*

    graphing, *c98*, 98–99

    in Great Smoky Mountains, *p113*

    niche for, 82

Positive charge (+), 375–376

Positive electric field, 377

Potato plants, 64, *p65*

Potential energy, 434, 448, *c449*

Precambrian Era, *c245*

Precipitation, 178, *c187*, 192

Predators

    adaptations to protect against, *c28*, 28–29

    in food chain, 86

Predict, 517, 527, 537, 543

Predicting, 38, 66, 67, 70, 101, 134, 166, 180, 201, 226, 227, 360, 361, 364, 395, 398, 430, 436, 451, 454, 474, 492, 510

Predicting weather, 196

Preservation of environment, 128–129

Prey, 86

Printing, c556

Prism, c422

Process Skills. *See* Science Process Skills

Producers, 84, 86

Properties

diagnostic, c250

of glue, 338–339

observed, c250

Protection, c28, c29

Protists, c11

Ptolemy, 544

Pulley, p458, c466, 466–467, c467, 476–477

Pumice, p246

Pyrite, p240, c241

Python, c18–c19, c20–c21

Quartz, p239, 240, c241

Quiz Show, 38, 70, 98, 134, 166, 206, 228, 254, 278, 342, 364, 398, 430, 454, 478, 510, 542, 566

Rabbit population, c98, 98–99

Radiation, p347, c358–c359

Radiators, c357

Radio waves, 418, c419

Rain

acid, 295

erosion by, 266

measuring, 195

Rain gauge, 195

Ramp, c468

Ratio, 564

Rays of light, 417

Reading Skills. *See* Target Reading Skills

Recycle, c132, 132–133, c283, c296, c297

technology and, 553

of water, 186–187

Red light, c418

Red Planet. *See* Mars

Red Sea, 185

Red wolves, p120–p121

Redwood trees, 47

Reflection, p402, c421

Refraction, 422

Relative motion, 434, 439

Renewable resources, 292

solar energy as, 292, 293

water as, 293

wind energy, c293

Renewable natural resources, 287

soil as, 288–291

water as, 300–301

Repelling of objects with same charge, 376

Reproduction

by plants, c16, c17, c54–c57

two-step cycle with spores, 62

Reptiles

body temperature of, c18

characteristics of, c18, 19

life cycle of, c20–c21

Resistance, 370, 379

Resistor in closed circuit, c379

Resources. *See* Natural resources

Respiratory system, 148, c149, 150

Revolution, 490, c498

Rigel (star), c505

Rings

of Saturn, 530, p531

of Uranus, p532

Rivers, 183, p184, 185

Roadrunner, p85

in food web, 88, c89

niche of, 82

Rock

changing into soil, 243

deposition and, 267

erosion and, 266

fossils in, c244, 244–245

igneous, c246, c247

metamorphic, c248

sedimentary, c242, c243

in soil, 289

Rock cycle, 248, c249

Roentgen, Wilhelm, 555

Roller coaster, c441

Root hairs, c52, c53

Roots, 47, 52

fibrous, c52

taproots, c53

Rotation, 490

of Earth, 496

of Uranus, 532

Rubber recycling, c296

Runners and new plants, c64, 65

Rust, c336

Safety in transportation, 559

Saffir-Simpson Hurricane Scale, c228, 228–229

Saguaro cactus, 80, 128

Saguaro National Park, p128

Saliva, p153, 156

Salt (ocean), 184–185, 330

Saltwater ecosystem, c91

San Andreas Fault, 273

Sand, c290, 291, c331

Sand dunes, 267

Sandstone, 243, p243

San Francisco earthquakes, 273

Satellites (artificial), 514

   communication, 557

   hurricane prediction with, c220

   solar energy for, 293

   space exploration and, 525

   weather observation by, 202–203

Satellites (moons). *See also* Moon, 524

Saturn, c520, p530

Scale, 564

Scale models and drawings, 564–565

Scales (plates) of reptiles, 19

Scavengers, 84, c85, 94

Science Fair Projects, 176, 312, 488, 576

Science Journal, 21, 53, 57, 61, 79, 93, 111, 123, 153, 263, 280, 287, 329, 335, 344, 351, 359, 377, 407, 425, 441, 445, 463, 497, 521, 525, 531, 551, 555

Science map, c213

Scientific methods, xxvi

Science Process Skills,

   Classifying, 34, 35, 38, 100, 236, 250, 278, 342, 455, 478

   Collecting Data, 108, 130, 131, 302, 338, 339, 450

   Communicating, 174, 180, 204, 311, 460, 475, 487, 575

   Estimating and Measuring, 201, 284, 308, 310, 360, 484, 516, 574

   Forming Questions and Hypotheses, 172, 231, 308, 484, 510, 566, 572

   Identifying and Controlling Variables, 172, 308, 572

   Inferring, 38, 66, 67, 70, 96, 97, 100, 131, 134, 140, 162, 163, 166, 204, 226, 230, 254, 260, 274, 275, 278, 284, 299, 316, 342, 348, 364, 372, 395, 398, 404, 426, 427, 454, 478, 510, 539, 542, 548, 560, 561

   Interpreting Data, 200, 201, 204, 431, 436, 451

   Investigating and Experimenting, 308, 339, 398, 474, 484, 572

   Making and Using Models, 162, 163, 212, 231, 298, 299, 364, 516, 538, 539, 548

   Making Operational Definitions, 394, 395

   Observing, 4, 44, 66, 67, 70, 76, 96, 97, 108, 130, 131, 134, 163, 174, 236, 250, 251, 260, 274, 275, 310, 316, 338, 339, 343, 348, 372, 394, 404, 426, 450, 485, 492, 506, 507, 560, 561

   Predicting, 38, 66, 67, 70, 101, 134, 166,180, 201, 226, 227, 360, 361, 364, 395, 398, 430, 436, 451, 454, 474, 492, 510

Scientific names, 12, c12

Screw, 458, c471

Screwdriver, p466

Sea breeze, 188

Seas, 183, p184

Seasons, 499, c499

Sea stars, 22

Sediment, p234, 242, c244

Sedimentary rock, p235, 242–243, c242–c243

   fossils in, c244, 244–245

   in rock cycle, c249

Sedna, p537

Seed cone, c16

Seedling, p59

Seeds, p60

   animal helpers to move, c61

   from conifers, c16

   in dormant state, 62

   from flowering plants, c16

   growing plants without, 66–67

   making of, 55

   plant growth and, 62

   in plant life cycle, c58

   water for moving, 61

   wind for moving, 60

Seneca, c425

Sepal, p42, p54, 55

Sequence, 77, 87, 95, 101, 437, 439, 443, 455

Series circuit, 370, c380

Set, 34–35

Shadows, c417, 496

Shells, 28

Shelter, 111

Shoreline erosion, 266

Silent Spring (Carson), 104

Silt, c290

Simple electric motor, c388–c389

Simple machines, 463
  Archimedes and, 480
  inclined plane, c468–c469
  lever, c464, c465
  pulley, p466–c467
  screw, c471
  wedge, c470
  wheel and axle, p466

Simpson, Joanne, 208

Simulations, 456

Sinking, 326–327, 340, 341

Skeletal muscles, c146, c147

Skeletal system, 144, c145

Skin, 156, c157

Slate, p248

Small intestine, c153

Smallpox vaccine, c160

Smith, Rebecca, p135

Smooth muscles, 147, c147

Snails, c24, c25

Snakes, c18–c19, p20, c21

Social Studies in Science
  11, 31, 63, 83, 90, 117, 129, 143, 159, 195, 215, 217, 271, 289, 331, 355, 375, 383, 413, 469, 495, 519, 557

Soil
  clay, p290
  for growing plants, 291
  ingredients in, 289
  qualities of, 290
  as renewable resource, 287, 288, 291
  rock changing into, 243
  sand, c290
  silt, c290
  uses of, 291

Solar cars, 304

Solar cell, p283, c292, 293

Solar Cookers International, 367

Solar eclipse, 490, c503

Solar energy, p282, 287, c292
  as power source, 473
  as renewable energy source, 292
  uses of, 293

Solar farm, 293

Solar heat system, 293

Solar panels, p292, 293

Solar system, 514, 519, c520

Solid (state of matter), 320, c321
  light traveling in, 422
  sound waves in, c410
  volume of, 323, c323

Solubility, p315, c331

Solute, p315, 330

Solution, p315, c330, c331

Solvent, p315, 330

Sonoran Desert, p128

Sound, 407
  loudness of, c412
  pitch of, c413
  speeds of, c411, c428, 428–429

Sound wave, 407
  compression, 408
  echoes and, 411
  frequency of, 409
  longitudinal, 408
  transverse, 408
  traveling by, 410
  wavelength of, c409

Southern Hemisphere, c499

Southern Ocean, c183, c184

South-seeking pole, c383

Soybean pod, c16

Space
  ecosystems in, 102–103
  exploration of, 525, p525
  transportation systems in, 559

Space engineer, 456

Space probe, 514, 522, c527

Spanish moss, 52, p52

Species, 12
  in animal kingdom, c13
  endangered, 120
  extinct, 120
  past and present, 121
  rapid changes and, 122
  threatened, 120

Speed, 434, 440, c441
  relating distance, time, and, 452–453
  of sounds, c428, 428–429

Sperm cells in pollen, 55

Sphagnum moss, 63

Spiders, 22, c22, 289

Spinal cord, 154, c155

Spiny skins, 28

Spirit (Mars probe), c527

Spore case, 16, 62, c63

Spores, 16, c16, c63
  in dormant state, 62
  plant growth and, 62
  two-step reproduction cycle with, 62

Spring (season), *499*

Spring scale, *p447*

Sputnik, *525*

Stamen, *p42, c54, 55, 56, 57*

Stars, *494, 495*

  characteristics of, *504*

  constellations (patterns) of, *c504, c505*

  Earth's rotation and, *496*

States of matter, *320, c321*

Static electricity, *370, 375, 400*

Steam power, *393*

Steel, *330, 350*

Stems, *c47, c51, 65*

Stoma, *p48, c51*

Stomach, *c153, c156*

Storage in water cycle, *c187*

Stored energy, *448, 449*

Storm surge, *210, c218, 219*

Stratus clouds, *c192, c193*

Strawberries, *p64, 65*

Streak of minerals, *c240*

Strep throat, *c159*

Strip mining, *p126*

Subsoil, *c289*

Succession, *p106, 118, 119*

Sugar, *c47*

Summarize, *237, 239, 241, 243, 245, 255, 461, 467, 473, 479*

Summer, *499*

Sun, *495. See also* Solar energy

  characteristics of, *521, p521*

  cooking with energy from, *367*

  Earth's revolution and, *493*

  Earth's rotation and, *496*

  as light source, *416*

  lunar eclipse and, *c502*

  midnight, *c499*

  planets' orbits around, *520*

  radiation and movement of energy from, *358, c359*

  solar eclipse and, *503, c503*

  in summer and winter skies, *c497*

  ultraviolet waves from, *418*

  water cycle and, *187*

Sunlight

  as energy source, *84*

  plant leaves and, *c50*

  plant responses to, *c68*

  for plants, *47*

  as resource, *286, c286*

Sunspots, *521*

Surface and friction, *445*

Surface Coal Mining Law, *127*

Surface Solar Energy (SSE) information, *367*

Swallowing, *c157*

Swamp ecosystems, *90, c91*

Swan, Joseph, *417*

Sweet potato plant, *45*

Switch in closed circuit, *c379*

System, *79, 217*

Table, *252, 508*

Table Mountain pine, *122*

Take-Home Activity, *37, 40, 69, 72, 99, 103, 104, 133, 136, 165, 168, 203, 207, 208, 229, 232, 253, 256, 277, 280, 301, 304, 341, 344, 363, 367, 368, 397, 400, 429, 432, 453, 456, 477, 480, 509, 512, 541, 544, 563, 567*

Tally Chart, *228, 476*

Taproots, *p53*

Target Reading Skills

  Cause and Effect, *109, 115, 121, 135, 181, 185, 189, 193, 205, 285, 291, 295, 303, 349, 353, 359, 364, 373, 379, 389, 399, 493, 499, 505, 511*

  Compare and Contrast, *5, 9, 17, 25, 39, 261, 265, 269, 279, 317, 321, 337, 343*

  Draw Conclusion, *45, 49, 65, 71, 141, 147, 157, 167, 405, 411, 415, 419, 425, 431*

  Main Idea and Details, *213, 221, 225, 231, 549, 553, 559, 565*

  Predict, *517, 527, 537, 543*

  Sequence, *77, 87, 95, 101, 437, 439, 443, 455*

  Summarize, *237, 239, 241, 243, 245, 255, 461, 467, 473, 479*

Tarnish, *c336*

Tears, *156*

Technology, *546*

  communication and, *556–557*

  definition of, *551*

  effect of, *551*

  environment and, *554*

  food and, *554*

  health and, *552, c553*

  materials and, *552*

  medicine and, *554–555*

  recycling and, *553*

  of time measurement, *559*

  transportation systems and, *558–559*

  Velcro® and, *552*

Technology in Science 33, 125, 161, 187

Teeth
human, c153
of machine, 472

Telecommunications, 546, c557

Telescopes, c424
Galileo and, 530
Hubble Space Telescope, c536
for looking at Sun, c521

Temperature
air pressure and, 188
effects on matter, c334–c335
graphing, c204, 205
vs. heat, 353
measuring, 194
solar energy effects on, 292
weathering and changes in, 264

Temperature scales, c362, 362–363

Terra **(satellite),** 202

Terraces, c269

Test Talk, 169, 305, 481, 569

Testing of matter, 319

Thales, 376, c392

Thermal energy, p346, 351, 353, p353, 354

Thermal Protection Materials and System Branch (NASA), 366

Thermogram, p351

Thermometer, c352

Threatened species, 120

Thunder, 375

Thunderstorms
cold front and, 192

hurricanes and, c216, 217, c218
tornadoes and, c222, 223
from tropical depression, c216

Time, 452–453

Timeline on use of lenses, c424–c425

Time measurement, 559

Tire recycling, c296

Tissues, c8
of human body, 143
of plants, 50

Tomato plant, 58

Topaz, 240

Topsoil, c289

Tornado, 210
compared to hurricane, 225
forecasting, 224, p224
formation of, c222–c223
hurricane and, c218
watches and warnings, 225

Torricelli, Evangelista, 194

TPS (Thermal Protection System) materials, 366

Trachea (windpipe), 148, c149

Tracking weather, c196–c197

Transcontinental jet service, c559

Transcontinental railroad, c558

Translucent, p402, 421

Transparent, p402, 421

Transpiration, c51

Transportation systems, c558–c559

Transverse waves, 408

Trees
climate information on, 198, c198
genus and, 12
as natural resource, 287
redwood, 47
stems of, c51

Triton (moon), 534, 535

Tropical depression, 210, c216

Tropical rain forests, 29, c81

Tropical storms, 215
names of, c219
stages of, 216

True bacteria, c11

Tsunamis, 273

Tuataras, 19

Tubelike vascular plant structures, c14

Tulips, 64

Tundra, p81

Tuning fork, c413

Ultraviolet waves, 418, c419

Universe, 514, 519

Upper mantle, 272

Uranus, c520, p532, c533

Vaccine, 139, c160, 161

Vacuum in outer space, 410

Variables. *See* Identifying and Controlling Variables

Vascular plants, 14

Vascular tissue, 14

Vehicle, 546, 558

Veins
in heart, c151
in plants, c47

Velcro®, 552
Velocity, 434, *c*441
Ventricle, 150, *c*151
Venus, *c*520, *p*523, *c*523
Vertebrates, 18–21
Vibrations, 407
Video cameras, *c*557
***Viking I* (Mars probe),** *c*527
Violet light, 418, *c*419
Violin, *c*413
Viruses, *c*9, 158, *c*159
Visible spectrum colors, 418
Volcanoes, *p*258, *c*270
    active and dormant, 271
    effects of, *c*273
    eruptions of, 270, *c*270
    on Mars, 527
    in rock cycle, *c*249
Volume, *c*324, *c*325
Voluntary muscles, *p*138, 146
Vortex, 210, 223
***Vostok I* (spacecraft),** 525
Voyager (space probe), 530

Wagon, *p*444–*p*445
Warm front, *c*192
Water
    deposition by, 267
    on Earth, 183
    energy from flowing, 293
    erosion by, 266
    formation of soil and, 288
    forms of, *c*318
    fresh, *c*184, 185
    as helper to move seeds, 61
    making fresh water from salt water, 180

as natural resource, 287
ocean, 330
phase changes in, *c*335
plants and, 14, 15, 47
salty, 184–185
in solar heat system, 293
states of, 183, *p*200, *c*201, 320, 321
use of, *c*300, 300–301
weather and, 186–187
weathering by, 264, *c*265
Water cycle, *c*186–*c*187, 292
Water ecosystems, *c*90, *c*91
Waterfowl adaptations, *c*26–*c*27
Water lilies, 47
Water pollution, 125
Water slide, *p*438
Waterspout, 223, *c*223
Water vapor, 183, 185, 188, 321
Wave, *p*406. *See also* Light wave; Sound wave
    erosion by, 266
    during hurricanes, *c*218, 219
    light, 418
    tsunamis, 273
Wavelength
    of light, 418
    of sound, *c*402, *c*409
Weather
    air and, 188–189, *c*190–*c*192
    climatic changes in, 198
    convection current and, 356
    measuring, 194–195
    observing from space, 202–203
    predicting, 196

tracking, 196–197
water and, 186–187
Weather charts, *c*196
Weather forecast, 196
Weathering, *p*259, 261, *c*264, *c*265
    chemical, 265
    deposition and, 267, 269
    erosion and, 266, 269
    gravity and, 268
    physical, 264
    soil renewal and, 288
Weather maps, *c*196, *c*197
Weather observation stations, 194
Weather radar, 196
Wedge, 458, *c*470
Weight and mass, 446, 447
Wetland ecosystems, 90
Wheel and axle, 458, *p*466
White blood cells, 161
White-crowned sparrows, 33
White marble, 239
Wind, 188
    deposition by, 267
    as helper to move seeds, 60
    of hurricane, *p*218, *c*218
    land breeze, *c*188
    measuring speed of, *c*195
    pollination by, 57
    to power generator, 393, *c*393
    sea breeze as, *c*188
Wind energy, *c*293
Wind farms, *c*392
Wind turbines, 393
Wind vane, 178, *c*194, 195
Wings, 29
Winter, 499
Wood, 355, *p*355

Woolly mammoths, 121

Work, 434

World Wide Web, 556

Wright, Orville and Wilbur, *c*558

Writing in Science

Descriptive, 123, 255, 263, 279, 303, 335, 351, 407, 441, 445, 455, 463, 521, 555

Expository, 13, 21, 39, 53, 57, 71, 79, 111, 135, 167, 205, 223, 329, 343, 359, 365, 385, 399, 425, 431, 479, 497, 511, 531, 551

Narrative, 61, 93, 153, 231, 273, 287, 377, 525

Persuasive, 101, 199, 293, 297, 471, 543, 565

X rays, 418, *c*419, *c*555

Year, 498

Yellowstone National Park, *p*128

You Are There!, 6, 46, 78, 110, 142, 182, 214, 238, 262, 286, 318, 350, 374, 406, 438, 462, 494, 518, 550

Zebras, *c*29, 32

Zooplankton, *p*92

Credits

Illustrations

8-32 Marcel Laverdet; 9, 43, 49, 57 Robert Ulrich; 80-94, 184-198, 352-359 Bop Kayganich; 106-128, 189, 380-383, 408-410, 419, 442, 500 Peter Bollinger; 216-224, 288, 294 Tony Randazzo; 242-244, 264-272 Alan Male.

Photographs

Every effort has been made to secure permission and provide appropriate credit for photographic material. The publisher deeply regrets any omission and pledges to correct errors called to its attention in subsequent editions.

Unless otherwise acknowledged, all photographs are the property of Scott Foresman, a division of Pearson Education.

Photo locators denoted as follows: Top (T), Center (C), Bottom (B), Left (L), Right (R), Background (Bkgd).

Cover:

(T) ©Gerry Ellis/Minden Pictures, (C) ©Lynn Stone/Index Stock Imagery, (Bkgd) ©ThinkStock/SuperStock, (BL) Rubberball Productions.

Front Matter:

i ©Lynn Stone/Index Stock Imagery; ii ©DK Images; iii (TR) Getty Images, (BR) ©Royalty-Free/Corbis; v ©Jerry Young/DK Images; vi (TL) ©Zig Leszczynski/Animals Animals/Earth Scenes, (B) ©DK Images; vii Getty Images; viii (CL) ©Breck P. Kent/Animals Animals/Earth Scenes, (BL) ©E. R. Degginger/Color-Pic, Inc.; ix ©Dr. Dennis Kunkel/Visuals Unlimited; x (TL) ©Steve Wilkings/Corbis, (BR) Getty Images; xi (TR) Getty Images, (B) Stephen Oliver/©DK Images; xii (TL) ©Ted Mead/PhotoLibrary, (BL) ©Hubert Stadler/Corbis; xiii ©Alan Schein Photography/Corbis; xiv (TL) PhotoLibrary, (BL) ©Charles O'Rear/Corbis; xv Digital Vision; xvi (TL) Getty Images, (BL) ©Alan Schein Photography/Corbis; xvii ©Royalty-Free/Corbis, (BL) ©DK Images; xviii (TL) ©Paul & Lindamarie Ambrose/Getty Images, (BL) ©Stocktrek/Corbis; xix ©Yang Liu/Corbis; xxii ©Stephanie Maze/Corbis; xxiii (BC) ©Bill Varie/Corbis, (TR, CR) NASA, (BR) ©Scott T. Smith/Corbis; xxiv ©Richard T. Nowtiz/Corbis, Gallaudet University; xxv (CL) ©DK Images, (BL) Stephen Oliver/©DK Images, (TR) ©Dr. Ray Weil, University of Maryland, (CR, BR) NASA; xxvi ©Richard T. Nowitz/Corbis; xxviii (CC) Brand X Pictures, (CC, BC) Getty Images; xxix (L, CR, BR) Getty Images; xxx (BL, R) Getty Images, (TL) Brand X Pictures, (TC) ©Leonard Lessin/Peter Arnold, Inc.; xxxi (TL) Brand X Pictures, (BC) Getty Images, (BR) ©Jim Cummins/Getty Images.

Unit A:

Divider: (Bkgd) ©Tim Flach/Getty Images, (CC) Digital Vision; Chapter 1: 1 (Bkgd) ©Zig Leszczynski/Animals Animals/Earth Scenes, (CR) ©Richard LaVal/Animals Animals/Earth Scenes; 2 (BL) ©Ken Cole/Animals Animals/Earth Scenes, (T) ©Martha J. Powell/Visuals Unlimited, (B) ©DK Images; 3 ©Ralph A. Clevenger/Corbis; 5 (CR) ©Gusto Productions/SPL/Photo Researchers, Inc., (Bkgd) ©Martha J. Powell/Visuals Unlimited; 6 ©Martha J. Powell/Visuals Unlimited; 8 (BR) ©Eye of Science/Photo Researchers, Inc., (TL) ©Carolina Biological/Visuals Unlimited, (CL) ©SIU/Visuals Unlimited, (BL) ©Alfred Pasieka/Photo Researchers, Inc.; 10 (BL) Getty Images, (CL) ©Stephen Dalton/NHPA Limited; 11 (TL) ©T. Beveridge/Visuals Unlimited, (TL) ©L. Stannard/Photo Researchers, Inc., (CL) ©Eric Grave/Phototake, (BL) ©Ken Cole/Animals Animals/Earth Scenes, (BL) ©Craig Tuttle/Corbis, (CL) ©Royalty-Free/Corbis; 12 (CL) ©Ken Cole/Animals Animals/Earth Scenes, (BCL) Getty Images, (TL) ©DK Images, (BL) ©Kevin Schafer/Corbis; 13 (TR, TC, TCR, BR) ©DK Images, (TCL) ©Ken Cole/Animals Animals/Earth Scenes, (TC) ©John Conrad/Corbis, (TCR) ©Ray Richardson/Animals Animals/Earth Scenes; 14 (BL) ©John Durham/Photo Researchers, Inc., (L) Sue Atkinson/©DK Images; 15 (BL) ©DK Images, (TL) Karl Shone/©DK Images, (CL) Lee W. Wilcox; 16 (BL) ©Wolfgang Kaehler/Corbis, (TL) Getty Images, (CL) ©DK Images; 17 (TC) ©Larry Lee/Corbis, (CC) ©Steve Terrill/Corbis, (T) Getty Images; 18 (CR, BL, TCL) ©DK Images, (CL) ©Jane Burton/DK Images, (TL) Getty Images, (BCL) ©Ray Richardson/Animals Animals/Earth Scenes; 19 ©DK Images; 20 (TR) ©Jim Tuten/Animals Animals/Earth Scenes, (CL, BR) ©DK Images; 21 (TR, B) ©DK Images; 22 (BL) ©Philip James Corwin/Corbis, (TR) ©DK Images; 23 (BC) Jerry Young/©DK Images, (CL) ©Andrew Syred/Photo Researchers, Inc., (BR) ©F. J. Jackson/Robert Harding Picture Library, Ltd., (TR) Dave King/©DK Images; 24 ©Kevin Summers/Getty Images; 25 (TL, CR, CL) ©Dwight R. Kuhn, (TR) ©Chase Swift/Corbis; 26 ©DK Images; 27 (TR) ©John Conrad/Corbis, (TL) ©Peter Johnson/Corbis, (BR) ©Jeffrey L. Rotman/Peter Arnold, Inc., (Bkgd) ©Stephen Frink; 28 (TL, CL) ©Ray Richardson/Animals Animals/Earth Scenes, (BR) ©DK Images, (BL) ©E. R. Degginger/Color-Pic, Inc.; 29 (B) Digital Stock, (CC) ©DK Images; 30 ©Ray Richardson/Animals Animals/Earth Scenes; 31 (TL) ©Ken Cole/Animals Animals/Earth Scenes, (BL) ©Steve Kaufman/Corbis, (CL) ©Ralph A. Clevenger/Corbis; 32 (TR) ©Eric Baccega/Nature Picture Library, (B) ©Anup Shah/Nature Picture Library; 33 ©Manoj Shah/Getty Images; 34 (TL) ©Martin B. Withers/Frank Lane Picture Agency/Corbis, (CL, BL) ©DK Images, (CL) ImageState, (TR) ©Lonny Kalfus/Getty Images; 35 (TL) ©Martin B. Withers/Frank Lane Picture Agency/Corbis, (TL, BL, B) ©DK Images, (CL) ImageState; 36 (Bkgd) ©Patti Murry/Animals Animals/Earth Scenes, (BL) ©DK Images; 37 (CL, BL) ©DK Images, (BC) Getty Images, (CC) ©John Gerlach/Animals Animals/Earth Scenes, (BR) Jerry Young/©DK Images, (CR) ©Science VU/Visuals Unlimited, (TR) Brand X Pictures; 39 ©DK Images; 40 (Bkgd) ©M. P. Kahl/Photo Researchers, Inc., (TL) NASA; 41 (TCL) Getty Images, (Bkgd) PhotoLibrary; Chapter 2: 42 (B) ©Royalty-Free/Corbis, (T) ©George D. Lepp/Corbis; 43 (BR) ©Carolina Biological Supply Company/Phototake, (BL) ©John Kaprielian/Photo Researchers, Inc.; 45 ©George D. Lepp/Corbis; 46 ©George D. Lepp/Corbis; 48 (TL) ©DK Images, (R) ©TH Foto-Werbung/Photo Researchers, Inc.; 49 ©Dr. Jeremy Burgess/Photo Researchers, Inc.; 50 (TL, CR) ©DK Images; 51 (BR, TR) ©DK Images, (CR) Getty Images; 52 (TL, BR) ©DK Images, (TL) ©Gary Moss/Getty Images, (BC) Brand X Pictures; 53 (BC) ©Carolina Biological/Visuals Unlimited, (CR) ©DK Images; 54 (CL, B) ©Royalty-Free/Corbis, (TL) ©DK Images; 55 (TL) ©David Sieren/Visuals Unlimited, (TR) ©Owaki-Kulla/Corbis; 56 (TR) ©W. Treat Davidson/Photo Researchers, Inc., (TL) ©DK Images, (TL, B) ©Merlin Tuttle/BCI/Photo Researchers, Inc.; 57 ©John Kaprielian/Photo Researchers, Inc.; 58 (TL, CL, BL, BC, BR) ©DK Images; 59 (L, BC) ©DK Images; 60 (CL) Stephen Oliver/©DK Images, (TL, BL) ©DK Images; 61 ©Merlin Tuttle/BCI/Photo Researchers, Inc.; 62 (TL) ©Ed Reschke/Peter Arnold, Inc., (CL) ©Carolina Biological Supply Company/Phototake, (BL) ©John Shaw/Tom Stack & Associates, Inc., (TL) ©DK Images; 63 (Bkgd) ©Dwight R. Kuhn, (TR) Neil Fletcher and Matthew Ward/©DK Images; 64 Eric L. Heyer/Grant Heilman Photography, (BCR) Brand X Pictures, (BCL, R) ©DK Images; 65 ©DK Images; 66 ©Joseph Devenney/Getty Images; 68 (CL) Brand X Pictures, (BL) ©DK Images, (Bkgd) Digital Vision; 71 ©Royalty-Free/Corbis; 72 (Bkgd) ©Neale Clark/Robert Harding Picture Library, Ltd., (TL) NASA; 73 ©Breck P. Kent/Animals Animals/Earth Scenes; Chapter 3: 74 (T) ©Andrew Brown/Ecoscene/Corbis, (BR) ©George H. H. Huey/Corbis, (BL) ©Kennan Ward/Corbis, (T) ©Breck P. Kent/Animals Animals/Earth Scenes; 75 (BR) ©Raymond Gehman/Corbis, (TR) ©Raymond Gehman/NGS Image Collection, (BL) ©Jim Brandenburg/Minden Pictures; 77 ©Andrew Brown/Ecoscene/Corbis; 78 ©Andrew Brown/Ecoscene/Corbis; 80 (CL) ©Andrew Brown/Ecoscene/Corbis, (BL) ©David Keaton/Corbis; 81 (CR) ©Steve Terrill/Corbis, (TR) ©Michael Townsend/Getty Images, (BR) ©David Muench/Corbis; 82 (TL) ©Steve Kaufman/Corbis, (BL) ©Konrad Wothe/Minden Pictures; 83 (C) ©Raymond Gehman/NGS Image Collection, (BR) ©Steve Kaufman/Corbis, (T) ©George H. H. Huey/Corbis, (BC) Getty Images, (BL) ©Buddy Mays/Corbis, (TC) ©Daryl Balfour/Getty Images; 84 ©Biophoto Associates/Photo Researchers, Inc.; 85 (TR) ©Frank Lane Picture Agency/Corbis, (CR) ©Joe McDonald/Corbis, (TL) ©John Gerlach/Animals Animals/Earth Scenes, (CL) ©D. Robert & Lorri Franz/Corbis, (BR) ©DK Images, (TC) ©Tim Fitzharris/Minden Pictures, (BL) ©George H. H. Huey/Corbis; 86 (BL) ©Buddy Mays/Corbis, (BR) ©Jeff Foott/Nature Picture Library, (BC) ©John Cancalosi/Nature Picture Library; 87 ©Sally A. Morgan/Corbis; 88 (TR) ©Stephen J. Krasemann/DRK Photo, (CC, BR) ©Kennan Ward/Corbis, (CL) ©Michael Llewellyn/Getty Images; 89 (BL) ©Kevin Schafer/Corbis, (TC) Getty Images, (CL) ©Steve Kaufman/Corbis, (BR) ©Michael & Patricia Fogden/Corbis; 90 (TL) ©Roland Birke/Peter Arnold, Inc., (CL) ©Stephen Dalton/NHPA Limited; 91 (TL) ©Randy Wells/Getty Images, (BR) ©Ralph White/Corbis, (TR) Getty Images, (BL) ©Georgette Douwma/Getty Images; 92 (BC) British Antarctic Survey/SPL/Photo Researchers, Inc., (BR) ©Royalty-Free/Corbis, (TL) ©W. Perry Conway/Corbis, (BL) ©Roland Birke/Peter Arnold, Inc., (TC) ©Stephen Dalton/NHPA Limited; 93 (TR) ©Joe McDonald/Corbis, (TL) ©Royalty-Free/Corbis, (CL) ©George D. Lepp/Corbis; 95 ©Raymond Gehman/Corbis; 96 ©John & Eliza Forder/Getty Images; 98 (Bkgd) ©Neil McIntyre/Getty Images, (BL) ©D. Robert & Lorri Franz/Corbis; 101 ©DK Images; 102 ©Roger Ressmeyer/Corbis; 104 (BR) ©Alan G. Nelson/Animals Animals/Earth Scenes, (L) ©Tom Edwards/Animals Animals/Earth Scenes, (TL) ©George Rinhart/Corbis; 105 (Bkgd) ©E. R. Degginger/Color-Pic, Inc., (TR) ©Michael Fogden/Animals Animals/Earth Scenes; Chapter 4: 106 ©Orion Press/Corbis; 107 (TR) ©Frank Blackburn/Ecoscene/Corbis, (BL) ©Sullivan & Rogers/Bruce Coleman, Inc., (BR) ©Barbara Von Hoffmann/Animals Animals/Earth Scenes; 109 ©Orion Press/Corbis; 110 ©Orion Press/Corbis; 112 (CC) ©David Muench/Corbis, (TL, C) Getty Images, (BR) Hans Neleman/Getty Images; 113 (CC) ©Lynda Richardson/Corbis, (CL) ©Art Wolfe/Getty Images, (TCL, CR) ©DK Images, (TCR) ©Gary W. Carter/Corbis; 114 ©Royalty-Free/Corbis; 115 ©Ron Austing/Frank Lane Picture Agency/Corbis; 116 (BL) ©David Muench/Corbis, (R) ©Jon Sparks/Corbis; 117 (TR) ©Frank Blackburn/Ecoscene/Corbis, (BR) AP/Wide World Photos; 120 (CL) ©Sullivan & Rogers/Bruce Coleman, Inc., (BL) ©DK Images; 121 (CR) ©DK Images, (L) ©Barbara Von Hoffmann/Animals Animals/Earth Scenes, (BR) ©Peter Scoones/SPL/Photo Researchers, Inc.; 122 (BR) ©Martin B. Withers/Frank Lane Picture Agency/Corbis, (CL) ©1999 Tom Bean/DRK Photo, (CR) ©Marty Cordano/DRK Photo; 123 ©Marty Cordano/DRK Photo; 124 ©Bettmann/Corbis; 125 ©Bettmann/Corbis; 126 (B) ©Adrian Lyon/Getty Images, (CR) ©Vince Streano/Corbis; 127 ©Bruce Hands/Getty Images; 128 (CL) Getty Images, (BL) ©Doug Sokell/Visuals Unlimited; 129 (TR) ©Ed Reschke/Peter Arnold, Inc., (CR) ©Myrleen Ferguson Cate/PhotoEdit; 130 ©George Gerster/Photo Researchers, Inc.; 132 (Bkgd) ©Steve Allen/Getty Images, (Inset) ©Alain Choisnet/Getty Images; 135 ©DK Images; 136 (BL) NASA, (Bkgd) ©Jerry Driendl/Getty Images; 137 ©Dr. Dennis Kunkel/Visuals Unlimited; Chapter 5: 138 (BR) ©Dr. Kari Lounatmaa/Photo Researchers, Inc.; 139 ©Dr. Donald Fawcett & E. Shelton/Visuals Unlimited; 141 (L) ©Dr. Donald Fawcett/Visuals Unlimited, (BC) ©Dr. Richard Kessel & Dr. Randy Kardon/Tissues and Organs/Visuals Unlimited, (CR) ©Prof. P. Motta/Univ. "La Sapienza"/Photo Researchers, Inc.; 142 (L) ©Dr. Donald Fawcett/Visuals Unlimited, (BC) ©Dr. Richard Kessel & Dr. Randy Kardon/Tissues and Organs/Visuals Unlimited, (CR) ©Prof. P. Motta/Univ. "La Sapienza"/Photo Researchers, Inc.; 144 (BL) ©CNRI/Photo Researchers, Inc., (CL) ©Science Photo Library/Photo Researchers, Inc.; 147 (CR) ©SPL/Photo Researchers, Inc., (TR) ©Innerspace Imaging/Photo Researchers, Inc., (BR) ©Dr. Donald Fawcett/Visuals Unlimited; 152 ©Reuters/Corbis; 155 ©Alfred Pasieka/Photo Researchers, Inc.; 156 ©Prof. P. Motta/University "La Sapienza"/Photo Researchers, Inc.; 157 (TR) ©Susumu Nishinaga/Photo Researchers, Inc., (C) ©Dr. Fred Hossler/Visuals Unlimited; 158 ©Dr. Kari Lounatmaa/Photo Researchers, Inc.; 159 (CR) ©Science Source/Photo Researchers, Inc., (TL) ©Dr. David M. Phillips/Visuals Unlimited; 160 (TL, CL, BCL, BL) ©Bettmann/Corbis; 161 ©Dr. Donald Fawcett & E. Shelton/Visuals Unlimited; 162 Getty Images; 164 (B, Bkgd) ©Scott Camazine/Photo Researchers, Inc., (Bkgd) ©Dr. Wolf Fahrenbach/Visuals Unlimited, (BL) ©Tim Flach/Getty Images; 165 Getty Images; 168 (B) ©Bettmann/Corbis, (TR, BR) Corbis; 170 (T) ©Martha J. Powell/Visuals Unlimited, (TC) ©George D. Lepp/Corbis, (C) ©Andrew Brown/Ecoscene/Corbis, (BC) ©Orion Press/Corbis, (B) ©Dr. Richard Kessel & Dr. Randy Kardon/Tissues and Organs/Visuals Unlimited; 172 ©Daniel Zupanc/NHPA Limited; 176 (CC) Jerry Young/©DK Images, (CC) Steve Gorton and Gary Ombler/©DK Images, (Bkgd) ©Pat O'Hara/Corbis; 177 ©Steve Wilkings/Corbis.

Unit B:

Divider: (Bkgd) ©Alan Kearney/Getty Images, (CC) Brand X Pictures; Chapter 6: 178 (BR) Getty Images, (BR) ©DK Images, (TL) ©Earth Satellite Corporation/Photo Researchers, Inc.; 179 (CR) ©David Lees/Corbis, (BL) ©DK Images, (TR) Stephen Oliver/©DK Images; 181 ©Earth Satellite Corporation/Photo Researchers, Inc.; 182 ©Earth Satellite Corporation/Photo Researchers, Inc.; 184 ©Tom Van Sant/Corbis; 186 ©Charles O'Rear/Corbis; 188 (TR, CR) ©DK Images; 189 ©Darwin Wiggett/Corbis; 190 ©DK Images; 192 ©DK Images; 194 (L) ©David Lees/Corbis, (TR) ©Leonard Lessin/Peter Arnold, Inc., (BR) Getty Images; 195 (TR) Stephen Oliver/©DK Images, (BR) ©DK Images; 198 ©DK Images; 199 ©British Antarctic Survey/Photo Researchers, Inc.; 200 ©Mark Lewis/Getty Images; 202 ©Layne Kennedy/Corbis; 203 ©Jim Craigmyle/Corbis; 205 ©DK Images; 206 AP/Wide World Photos; 207 (BR) KSC/NASA, (Bkgd, BL) NASA; 208 (TL) Fritz Hoelzl/NOAA, (Bkgd) ©Jim Brandenburg/Minden Pictures; 209 (CL, Bkgd) Getty Images; Chapter 7: 210 (B) ©DK Images, (T) ©Reuters/Corbis; 211 (TR, CR) ©Japan Meteorological Agency, (BR, BL) ©Storm Productions, Inc.; 213 ©Reuters/Corbis; 214 ©Reuters/Corbis; 216 (BL, TL, CL, BR) ©Japan Meteorological Agency; 217 ©Adastra/Getty Images; 218 ©DK Images; 219 (CL) ©Cameron Davidson, (TL) ©Morton Beebe/Corbis; 220 (TL, BR) NASA, (BL) NASA/JPL; 222 (BL, BR) ©Storm Productions, Inc.; 223 (BL) ©Storm Productions, Inc., (CR) ©H. Hoflinger/FLPA-Images of Nature, (TR) ©ANT Photo Library/NHPA Limited; 224 (R) ©Reuters/Corbis, (CL) ©Jim Reed/Photo Researchers, Inc.; 228 (BC, Bkgd) Corbis; 231 NASA; 232 (BR) ©Chris Sattlberger/Photo Researchers, Inc., (TR) Albion Historian; 233 (Bkgd) ©Ted Mead/PhotoLibrary, (TC) ©DK Images; Chapter 8: 234 ©Adam Jones/Photo Researchers, Inc.; 235 (TC, TR, BL, CR, CC) ©DK Images, (BR) Richard M. Busch; 237 (CR) ©Judith Miller/©DK Images, (Bkgd) ©Adam Jones/Photo Researchers, Inc.; 238 ©Adam Jones/Photo Researchers, Inc.; 239 (TR, CR) ©DK Images, (BR) GeoScience Resources/American Geological Institute; 240 (BC, BCL, TR, BL, CL, TL) ©DK Images, (TL, BR) ©Colin Keates/Courtesy of the Natural History Museum, London/DK Images; 241 (CL) ©Colin Keates/Courtesy of the Natural History Museum, London/DK Images, (TL, TR, BR, BL, BC, CC) ©DK Images, (CL) Natural History Museum/©DK Images; 242 (TL, CL) ©DK Images; 243 (TR, BR) ©DK Images, (CR) Dave King/©DK Images; 244 (TR) Harry Taylor/Courtesy of the Natural History Museum, London/©DK Images, (TL, BR) ©Danny Lehman/Corbis; 246 (BL, CL, TL) ©DK Images; 247 (L) Alan Williams/©DK Images, (TR, TC) ©DK Images, (TL) Colin Keates/Courtesy of the Natural History Museum, London/©DK Images; 248 (TL, CL) ©DK Images, (TL, BL) Richard M. Busch; 252 Royalty-Free/Corbis; 253 (L) Digital Vision, (R) ©Bob Thomason/Getty Images, (TL) ©Barry Runk/Grant Heilman Photography, (TL) ©Andrew J. Martinez/Photo Researchers, Inc.; 255 Richard M. Busch; 256 (BL, BC, TR) JPL/NASA, (TR) NASA; 257 ©Hubert Stadler/Corbis; Chapter 9: 258 (T) ©Art Wolfe/Getty Images, (BR) ©Chris Reynolds and the BBC Team-Modelmakers/DK Images, (BL) ©Paul A. Souders/Corbis; 259 ©Jack Dykinga/Getty Images; 261 (CR) ©Owaki-Kulla/Corbis, (Bkgd) ©Art Wolfe/Getty Images; 262 ©Art Wolfe/Getty Images; 264 AP/Wide World Photos; 265 ©Jack Dykinga/Getty Images; 267 ©Owaki-Kulla/Corbis; 268 ©Paul A. Souders/Corbis; 269 (TR) ©Dave G. Houser/Corbis, (CR) ©Richard Bickel/Corbis; 270 ©Chris Reynolds and the BBC Team-Modelmakers/DK Images; 271 (TR, CR, BR) ©Gary Rosenquist; 273 (TL) ©George Hall/Corbis, (CT) ©Getty Images; 274 ©Roger Ressmeyer/Corbis; 276 (Bkgd) ©James Balog/Getty Images, (BR) ©Baron Wolman/Getty Images; 277 ©David Weintraub/Science Source/Photo Researchers, Inc.; 279 ©Chris Reynolds and the BBC Team-Modelmakers/DK Images; 280 (Bkgd) ©Ralph White/Corbis, (TL) NOAA; 281 ©Alan Schein Photography/Corbis; Chapter 10: 282 (T) ©Layne Kennedy/Corbis, (BR) ©Charles E. Rotkin/Corbis, (B) ©Charles O'Rear/Corbis; 283 (CR) ©Kevin Burke/Getty Images; 284 ©Owaki-Kulla/Corbis, (TL) Clive Streeter/©DK Images; 285 ©Layne Kennedy/Corbis; 286 ©Layne Kennedy/Corbis; 289 (R) ©Deborah Kopp/Visuals Unlimited, (TL) Clive Streeter/©DK Images, (TR) Jerry Young/©DK Images, (TC) ©DK Images; 290 (B) ©Sylvain Saustier/Corbis, (TC) ©DK Images, (CR) Colin Keates/Courtesy of the Natural History Museum/©DK Images, (TR) Andreas Einsiedel/©DK Images; 291 (TR) ©Robert van der Hilst/Corbis, (CR) Ivor Kerslake/The British Museum/©DK Images; 292 (TL) AP/Wide World Photos, (B) ©Kevin Burke/Getty Images; 293 (TR) ©Royalty-Free/Corbis, (R) Corbis; 295 ©Charles E. Rotkin/Corbis; 296 (CR) ©Getty Images, (BC) ©Ricki Rosen/Saba/Corbis, (TR) ©Liz Hymans/Corbis, (TL) ©Owaki-Kulla/Corbis; 297 (B) ©Owaki-Kulla/Corbis, (TL) ©Carin Krasner/Corbis, (CL) ©Royalty-Free/Corbis; 298 ©Lucidio Studio, Inc./Corbis; 300 (Bkgd) ©Royalty-Free/Corbis, (BR, BC) Getty Images, (CC) ©Frederik Astier/Sygma/Corbis, (CL) Brand X Pictures; 303 ©Kevin Burke/Corbis; 304 (TL, BL) AP/Wide World Photos; 306(TL) ©Earth Satellite Corporation/Photo Researchers, Inc., (BCL) ©Adam Jones/Photo Researchers, Inc., (TCL) ©Art Wolfe/Getty Images, (TCL) ©Sygma/Corbis; 307 (TR) Dave King/©DK Images, (TL) Layne Kennedy/Corbis; 309 ©Niall Benvie/Corbis; 312 (TC) Tom Ridley/©DK Images, (CC) ©DK Images, (Bkgd) ©Image Source Limited; 313 PhotoLibrary.

Unit C:

Chapter 11: 314 (T) ©Kevin Schafer/Getty Images, (BL) ©DK Images; 315 ©Royalty-Free/Corbis; 317 ©Kevin Schafer/Getty Images; 318 ©Kevin Schafer/Getty Images; 320 ©Bernhard Edmaier/Photo Researchers, Inc.; 326 ©DK Images; 327 ©DK Images; 329 ©DK Images; 330 ©Hans Neleman/Getty Images; 335 (TR, CR, BR) Science Museum, London/Corbis; 336 (R, BL) ©DK Images, (BL) Corbis, (CL) ©Royalty-Free/Corbis; 337 ©DK Images; 338 ©DK Images; 340 (R) ©Richard Megna/Fundamental Photographs; 342 ©Richard Laird/Getty Images; 343 ©DK Images; 344 (BL) JPL/NASA, (L) ©Cris Cordeiro/PhotoLibrary, (TL) Kennedy Space Center/NASA; 345 (CR) ©Royalty-Free/Corbis, (B) ©Charles O'Rear/Corbis; Chapter 12: 346 ©William Taufic/Corbis; 347 (BR) ©Chris Andrews Publications/Corbis, (BL) Stephen Oliver/©DK Images; 349 (CR) Getty Images, (Bkgd) ©William Taufic/Corbis; 350 ©William Taufic/Corbis; 351 ©A. Pasieka/Photo Researchers, Inc.; 352 Brand X Pictures; 355 (BR) ©Yann Arthus-Bertrand/Corbis, (CR) ©DK Images; 356 Stephen Oliver/©DK Images; 357 (C) ©Paul Seheult/Eye Ubiquitous/Corbis, (TR) ©Vera Storman/Getty Images; 358 (BL) ©Chris Andrews Publications, (TR) ©DK Images; 360 ©Stone/Getty Images; 362 (B) Getty Images, (T) ©Christoph Burki/Getty Images; 363 ©Paul Seheult/Eye Ubiquitous/Corbis; 366 (Bkgd) ©Craig Aurness/Corbis, (BR) ©Mark Edwards/Peter Arnold, Inc.; 367 Corbis; 368 (BR) ©Bettmann/Corbis, (L) ©Stephen Simpson/Getty Images; 369 Digital Vision; Chapter 13: 370 ©Byron Aughenbaugh/Getty Images; 371 ©Cordelia Molloy/Photo Researchers, Inc., (TR) ©DK Images; 373 ©Byron Aughenbaugh/Getty Images; 374 ©Byron Aughenbaugh/Getty Images; 376 (R) ©DK Images, (R) Clive Streeter/©DK Images; 378 ©Cameron/Corbis; 379 ©Richard Megna/Fundamental Photographs, (TR) ©DK Images; 382 ©Cordelia Molloy/Photo Researchers, Inc.; 383 (TR, CR, BR) ©Loren Winters/Visuals Unlimited; 385 ©Kennan Ward/Corbis; 386 (BL, BR) Andy Crawford/©DK Images; 388 (BL, TR) ©DK Images; 389 Dave King/Courtesy of The Science Museum, London/©DK Images; 391 (TR) ©Sheila Terry/Photo Researchers, Inc.; 392 (TL) ©New York Public Library/Photo Researchers, Inc.; ©George Bernard/Photo Researchers, Inc., (TC, CL) ©Science Photo Library/Photo Researchers, Inc., (BCL) The Granger Collection, NY, (CC) ©DK Images, (BL) Science & Society Picture Library; 393 (TL) Getty Images, (B) ©Royalty-Free/Corbis; 394 ©Jeremy Walker/Photo Researchers, Inc.; 396 Age Fotostock; 398 ©Cameron/Corbis; 400 (TL) The Granger Collection, NY, (CR) Getty Images, (BL) Age Fotostock; 401 (CC) ©Cooperphoto/Corbis, (R) ©Cameron/Corbis, (Bkgd) Getty Images; Chapter 14: 402 ©NOAO/Photo Researchers, Inc.; 403 (BL, BR) ©DK Images, (TR) ©Southern Illinois University Biomedical Communications/Custom Medical Stock Photo; 405 (CR) Getty Images, (Bkgd) ©Spencer Jones/Getty Images; 406 ©Spencer Jones/Getty Images; 407 Getty Images; 413 (TL, BL) Getty Images, (TR, CL) ©DK Images; 414 (TR, CR, BR) ©DK Images, (CR) Getty Images; 415 (CL) Getty Images, (TR) ©Bo Veisland, Mi & I/Photo Researchers, Inc.; 416 (BL) ©Chris Bjornberg/Photo Researchers, Inc., (BR) ©DK Images; 417 (TL) The Science Musuem/©DK Images, (BL) Mike Dunning/©DK Images; 418 (CR) ©Anthony Meshkinyar/Getty Images, (TL) Maxine Hall/Corbis; 419 ©Maxine Hall/Corbis, (CL) ©Adina Tovy/Robert Harding Picture Library, Ltd.; 420 ©Andy Crawford/Courtesy of the Football Museum, Preston/©DK Images, (R) ©NOAO/Photo Researchers, Inc., (CR) Steve Gorton and Kari Shone/©DK Images; 422 (TL) ©Southern Illinois University Biomedical Communications/Custom Medical Stock Photo, (TL) ©David Parker/Photo Researchers, Inc.; 423 (Bkgd) ©David Parker/Photo Researchers, Inc., (CR) Getty Images; 424 (TR, CR) ©E. R. Degginger/Color-Pic, Inc., (BL) Dave King/Courtesy of The Science Museum, London/©DK Images, (BCL) Peter Anderson/Courtesy of Saxon Village Crafts, Battle, East Sussex/©DK Images, (BC) ©DK Images, (BR) National Maritime Museum /©DK Images; 425 (CL) Getty Images, (TR) ©Matthew Borkoski/Index Stock Imagery, (CL) ©Bettmann/Corbis, (BL, BCR) ©Science Photo Library/Photo Researchers, Inc., (BR) Dave King/Courtesy of The Science Museum, London/©DK Images; 428 (CL) ©Steve Taylor/Getty Images, (BL) Getty Images, (BL, CL) AP/Wide World Photos, (Bkgd) ©Ulf Wallin/Getty Images, (BL) Corbis, (CL) ©Alan Smith/Getty Images; 429 AP/Wide World Photos; 431 ©DK Images; 432 (B, Bkgd) ©Royalty-Free/Corbis; 433 ©Alan Schein Photography/Corbis; Chapter 15: 434 (T) ©Scott T. Smith/Corbis, (BL) ©Robin Smith/Getty Images, (BR) ©Bill Bachman/PhotoEdit; 435 (BL) ©Jim Craigmyle/Corbis, (BR) ©Michael S. Lewis/Corbis; 437 ©Scott T. Smith/Corbis; 438 ©Scott T. Smith/Corbis; 439 Getty Images; 440 (TCL) ©Jim Craigmyle/Corbis, (CL) ©Tom & Dee Ann McCarthy/Corbis, (TL) ©Robin Smith/Getty Images, (BL) ©Raymond Gehman/Corbis;

441 ©Robin Smith/Getty Image; 442 ©DK Images; 443 (C) Jane Burton/©DK Images, (TR) ©DK Images, (TL, B) ©Bill Bachman/PhotoEdit; 445 ©Stanley R. Shoneman/Omni-Photo Communications, Inc.; 446 (BL) ©World Perspectives/Getty Images, (TR, TL) ©DK Images; 447 (TL) ©Bettmann/Corbis, (TL) ©Royalty-Free/Corbis; 448 (TR) ©Michael S. Lewis/Corbis, (TL) ©John Lund/Getty Images, (TL) ©Royalty-Free/Corbis; 449 (TR) ©Royalty-Free/Corbis, (BR) Jane Burton/©DK Images, (BR) ©Bettmann/Corbis; (BR) ©Peter Langone/Getty Images; 450 ©FotoKIA/Index Stock Imagery; 452 ©Lester Lefkowitz/Corbis; 453 ©Connie Ricca/Corbis; 455 Jane Burton/©DK Images; 456 (BL, BR, TL) NASA; 457 ©Royalty-Free/Corbis; Chapter 16: 458 (T) Digital Vision, (BL) ©DK Images, (BR) ©Lester Lefkowitz/Corbis; 459 ©Tony Freeman/PhotoEdit, (BL) ©DK Images, (BC) Getty Images; 461 (CR) ©Bob Krist/Corbis, (Bkgd) Digital Vision; 462 Digital Vision; 464 (CL, BL, TL) ©DK Images; 465 (TR, BR, CR) ©DK Images, (Bkgd) Getty Images; 466 (TR, TL) Getty Images, (CR) ©Tony Freeman/PhotoEdit, (BR) Brand X Pictures, (BR) Andy Crawford/©DK Images; 467 (TR) ©DK Images, (L) ©Paul Almasy/Corbis, (Bkgd) ©James P. Blair/Corbis; 468 ©Lester Lefkowitz/Corbis; 469 (T) Peter Arnold, Inc., (B) Getty Images; 470 (BL) ©DK Images, (R) ©Joe McBride/Getty Images; 471 (CR) ©DK Images; 472 (BR) ©David Vaughan/Photo Researchers, Inc., (CL) Brand X Pictures, (CL, BL) Getty Images; 473 (TR) Corbis, (TL) Getty Images, (TL, BL) Getty Images, (BL) Brand X Pictures; 474 ©Jeff Greenberg/Index Stock Imagery; 476 (Bkgd) ©John Noltner/Aurora Photos ©Keith Pritchard/Alamy Images; 478 (BR) Philip Gatward/©DK Images, (CR) Steve Gorton and Gary Ombler/©DK Images, (BC) Getty Images, (BCR) ©DK Images, (BR) ©Fukuhara, Inc./Corbis; 479 ©DK Images; 480 (BR) ©Hulton-Deutsch Collection/Corbis, (Bkgd) ©Alan Towse/Ecoscene/Corbis; 482 (TL) ©Kevin Schafer/Getty Images, (TCL) ©William Taufic/Corbis, (R) ©Byron Aughenbaugh/Getty Images, (BCL) ©Spencer Jones/Getty Images, (BL) ©Scott T. Smith/Corbis; 483 Digital Vision; 484 ©Steven E. Frishling/Sygma/Corbis; 488 (TC) Stephen Oliver/©DK Images, (Bkgd) ©DK Images, (Bkgd) ©Paul & Lindamarie Ambrose/Getty Images.

Unit D:

Divider: (Bkgd) NASA; Chapter 17: 490 ©Mark Garlick/Photo Researchers, Inc.; 491 (BL) ©Adrian Neal/Getty Images, (BR) Royal Greenwich Observatory/©DK Images; 493 (CR) GSFC/NASA, (Bkgd) ©David Parker/Photo Researchers, Inc.; 494 ©David Parker/Photo Researchers, Inc.; 496 ©John Sanford/Photo Researchers, Inc.; 498 (B) ©Arnulf Husmo/Getty Images, (TR) ©John Sanford/Photo Researchers, Inc.; 500 ©John Sanford/Photo Researchers, Inc.; 501 ©John Sanford/Photo Researchers, Inc.; 502 (B) ©Mark Garlick/Photo Researchers, Inc., (Bkgd) ©David Nunuk/Photo Researchers, Inc., (TL) ©John Sanford/Photo Researchers, Inc.; 503 (CL) ©G. Antonio Milani/Photo Researchers, Inc., (TL) ©Adrian Neal/Getty Images, (TR) ©David Parker/Photo Researchers, Inc., (CR) ©Mark Garlick/Photo Researchers, Inc., (Bkgd) Magrath Photography/Photo Researchers, Inc.; 504 (TR) Royal Greenwich Observatory/©DK Images, (TL) ©John Sanford/Photo Researchers, Inc.; 505 (CL) Royal Greenwich Observatory/©DK Images; 508 ©Roger Ressmeyer/Corbis; 508 ©Galen Rowell/Corbis; 511 ©G. Antonio Milani/Photo Researchers, Inc.; 512 (CL) NASA, (Bkgd) ©Fotopic/Index Stock Imagery; 513 ©Stocktrek/Corbis; Chapter 18: 514 (T) ©A. Morton/Photo Researchers, Inc., (B) ©USGS/Photo Researchers, Inc., (BL) JPL/NASA; 517 (CR) ©Bettmann/Corbis, (Bkgd) ©A. Morton/Photo Researchers, Inc.; 518 ©A. Morton/Photo Researchers, Inc.; 520 ©NASA/Photo Researchers, Inc.; 522 (TR) ©USGS/Photo Researchers, Inc., (BL) JPL/NASA; 523 JPL/NASA; 524 (CT, TR) Getty Images; 525 JSC/NASA; 526 (TR) U.S. Geological Survey, (Bkgd) NASA, (TL) JPL/NASA; 527 JPL/NASA; 528 (BR) JPL/NASA, (TL, CR) NASA; 529 (TL) Getty Images, (CL, BL) NASA, (CC) JPL/NASA; 530 (CL) ©Scala/Art Resource, NY, (TL) JPL/NASA, (TR) NASA, (BL, CC, BC, BR) ©Calvin Hamilton Solar Views, (BC) NASA, (BL) Tyson Boles; 531 (T, Bkgd) ©Mark Garlick/Photo Researchers, Inc.; 533 JPL/NASA; 534 (L) JPL/NASA, (TR) ©Mark Garlick/Photo Researchers, Inc., (B) ©NASA/Roger Ressmeyer/Corbis; 535 ©James King-Holmes/Photo Researchers, Inc., (BL) ©Mark Garlick/Photo Researchers, Inc., (CR) ©NASA/Photo Researchers, Inc.; 536 (TL) ©Bettmann/Corbis, (BC) ©NASA/Corbis, (BR, TL) JPL/NASA, (TR) NASA; 537 (BL) ©Mark Garlick/Photo Researchers, Inc., (R) ©Jet Propulsion Laboratory/NASA Image Exchange; 540 (CL) ©USGS/Photo Researchers, Inc., (CL, BL) JPL/NASA, (CL, BL) Getty Images, (BL) ©Comstock Inc., (BL) NASA, (Bkgd) ©Royalty-Free/Corbis; 542 ©Mark Garlick/Photo Researchers, Inc.; 543 JPL/NASA; 544 (TL) The Granger Collection, NY, (BL) ©Jim Ballard/Getty Images; 545 (TR) ©Royalty-Free/Corbis, (Bkgd) ©Yang Liu/Corbis; Chapter 19: 546 (T) ©Tibor Bognar/Corbis, (BR) ©DK Images, (BL) ©Ted Horowitz/Corbis; 547 Getty Images; 549 (CR) ©Stevie Grand/Photo Researchers, Inc., (Bkgd) ©Tibor Bognar/Corbis; 550 (Bkgd) ©Tibor Bognar/Corbis, (BR) ©Ted Soqui/Corbis; 552 (BL) ©J. Burgess/Photo Researchers, Inc.; 552 (TL) ©Donald Specker/Animals Animals/Earth Scenes, (CT) Getty Images; 553 Getty Images; 554 (BR) ©Simon Jauncey/Getty Images, (TL) ©Stevie Grand/Photo Researchers, Inc., (TC) ©Ted Horowitz/Corbis; 555 (L) ©Matt Meadows/Peter Arnold, Inc., ©James King-Holmes/Photo Researchers, Inc.; 556 (CR) ©DK Images, (R) Dave King/©DK Images, (TL) ©David Young-Wolff/PhotoEdit; 557 (TR) ©Courtesy of the Museum of the Moving Image, London/©DK Images, (TL) Tina Chambers/Courtesy of the National Maritime Museum, London/©DK Images, (TL) ©DK Images; 558 (CC, CR, CL, BL) ©Bettmann/Corbis, (BL) ©Archive Holdings, Inc./Getty Images, (BC) George H. Huey Photography, Inc.; 559 (CC) ©Museum of Flight/Corbis, (CR) Getty Images, (BR) ©Claro Cortes IV/Reuters/Corbis, (BC) ©Reuters/Corbis, (BL) Dave King/Courtesy of the Science Museum, London/©DK Images; 560 ©Chuck Swartzell/Visuals Unlimited; 562 (Bkgd) ©Roger Ball/Corbis, (BR) ©General Motors Corp. used with permission, GM Media Archives, (BC) Hughes Electronics Corporation; 565 ©David Young-Wolff/PhotoEdit; 566 (R, L) JPL/NASA; 567 (TR) GRIN/NASA Image Exchange, (CR) MSFC/NASA, (BR) Hubble Heritage Team/NASA; 568 (TL) The African American Registry®, (Bkgd) Getty Images, (CL) Medtronic, Inc.; 570 (TL) ©David Parker/Photo Researchers, Inc., (CL) ©A. Morton/Photo Researchers, Inc., (BL) ©Tibor Bognar/Corbis; 576 (BC) Mike Dunning/©DK Images, (Bkgd) NASA.

End Sheets:

©Steve Bloom Images/Alamy Images.